Jack Nicklaus

MEMORIES AND MEMENTOS

from Golf's Golden Bear

Jack Nicklaus

MEMORIES AND MEMENTOS

from Golf's Golden Bear

by **JACK NICKLAUS**

with **DAVID SHEDLOSKI**

Stewart, Tabori & Chang   New York

Published in 2007 by Stewart, Tabori & Chang
An imprint of Harry N. Abrams, Inc.

Produced by becker&mayer!, LLC., Bellevue, Washington
www.beckermayer.com

Design: Todd Bates
Editorial: Brian Arundel
Image Research: Shayna Ian and Lisa Metzger
Production Coordination: Leah Finger
Project Management: Sheila Kamuda

Library of Congress Cataloging-in-Publication Data

Nicklaus, Jack.
Jack Nicklaus : memories and mementos from golf's Golden Bear / by
Jack Nicklaus with David Shedloski.
    p. cm.
 ISBN-13: 978-1-58479-564-3
 ISBN-10: 1-58479-564-6
 1. Nicklaus, Jack. 2. Golfers--United States--Biography. I. Shedloski, David S. II. Title.

GV964.N5N53 2007
796.352092--dc22
[B]

2006021026

Manufactured in China

10 9 8 7 6 5 4 3 2 1

HNA
harry n. abrams, inc.
a subsidiary of La Martinière Groupe
115 West 18th Street
New York, NY 10011
www.hnabooks.com

CONTENTS

INTRODUCTION

WHEN A MUSEUM BEARING MY NAME OPENED IN 2002 IN MY HOMETOWN OF COLUMBUS, Ohio, on the campus of my beloved Ohio State University, it was one of the most overwhelming and humbling experiences of my life.

But the Jack Nicklaus Museum is far from being merely a well-appointed warehouse for the trophies and mementos my family and friends have collected throughout my career in the greatest game of all. I have tried to live my life to the fullest—according to principles that I have appreciated and respected far more than good golf shots. Also, I've always been a sort of historical sentimentalist, for lack of a better term; that is, the traditions of the game, and the integrity and purity of the sport, have been of utmost importance to me ever since I was introduced to golf as an eager ten-year-old who loved a good challenge.

I think one of the little jokes I made right around the time that the museum was ready to open was that I was sure glad my mother, Nellie Helen Nicklaus, and my wife, Barbara, were such good pack rats. It was my way of saying that I truly appreciated the care and thoughtfulness they put into the task of collecting items of importance to me and to people around me throughout the years.

That my mom began such a practice when I was a child, obviously long before I realized any measure of success with a golf club, is something at which I still marvel. She couldn't have possibly had that much foresight, as sharp as she was, to know that I would be so fortunate to go on and enjoy such a wonderful career, one that has enriched me and my family far beyond any monetary gain, championships, or accolades. What it really reflects is the love a mother has for her son. It's the same kind of love my father, Charlie, showed me, in addition to the encouragement he gave me—first as I was growing up, and then later as I applied myself to being the best golfer I could be.

Barbara, of course, was a willing accomplice in all of this squirreling away of items large and small, but her contributions to the museum pale in comparison to her role as my loving partner and best friend. She is someone who has always been there for me and has meant so much to my life and my career. I think it's obvious that those who have achieved some level of success in life didn't get there without tremendous support from the people most important to them, and that's something with which I have always been blessed. The museum is, in my mind, a testament to that support.

The reason this book was written was the hope that we could share with golf fans and nongolf fans alike not so much the items that have been collected, but the memories that go along with them, and how those memories were made possible. We thought it would be fun to share with readers a bit more about my career and life, and even share with them a few carefully selected mementos.

I'm grateful for the things I was able to enjoy because of the game of golf. That being said, golf was never as important to me as my wife and children and my growing family that today includes nineteen grandchildren. They are my real major championships.

What you'll find in these pages is evidence of a life that I hope you will recognize was about much more than just a game. An undeniable fact is that I have been a lucky man, blessed to a degree that I wish everyone could be blessed.

I hope you enjoy reading about this journey as much as I enjoyed living it. I think it would make Barbara smile to know that you found this collection of stories and artifacts worthwhile—entertaining and fun, and maybe even a bit like going to a museum. I'm certain that would have made my mom happy, too. After all, they did most of the work in helping me pull this together.

Jack Nicklaus

North Palm Beach, Florida

April 2006

CHARLIE NICKLAUS

THE FAMOUS ANKLE INJURY.

My father is really the author of the story about how I got my start in golf—how he hurt his ankle, took up the game as therapy, and how he dragged his ten-year-old son along as a caddie and sometime playing partner at Scioto Country Club. From those beginnings, a golfer was born.

Hardly. Any opportunity to talk about my father, Louis Charles Nicklaus, and the influence he had on my life and my golf career wouldn't start with that fragile joint in his leg, but rather with the strength of his character and the parts of his anatomy that made him such a wonderful father and person: his huge heart, his incredible spirit, his selflessness, his unswerving integrity, and his unquestionable support.

My dad was my best friend and I admired him more than anyone I've ever known. He died far too young for someone who loved life and the people around him so much. It's with a bit of wonder that I realize that I am ten years older, as I write this book, than he was when he died. My dad was fifty-six when he passed from cancer of the liver and pancreas in 1970, and there isn't a day that goes by that I don't think of him. As I grew up, I spent more time with him than I did

My dad taught me a lot about golf, and a lot more about life. I still miss him every day. Previous: My approach shot on the 18th hole in the first round of the 2004 Memorial Tournament.

anyone else, simply because he wanted to spend time with me. He believed in me, supported the things I did, and he was always there for me, whether I needed a boost or a kick in the rear end. He rarely offered unsolicited advice about my golf game, but he was always there if I asked. I can't think of too many times when I didn't seek his counsel on important decisions, be it family, golf, business, or other matters away from the course. I can't think of any, really.

A former semipro football player after graduating from Ohio State in 1935, and a fine all-around athlete growing up, my dad idolized Bob Jones, so my idol was Jones. He had watched Jones play in the 1926 U.S. Open at Scioto Country Club, and when I was growing up I heard all the stories about Jones, where he hit particular shots, what he did on the way to winning that championship. I haven't told this story often, but it was one of my dad's favorite tales because it further tied him to Jones. The 1931 Ryder Cup was staged at Scioto, and Jones was there. My dad walked up to the clubhouse and a policeman at the door asked my father, "Where would you like to go, Mr. Jones?" He kind of looked like Bob Jones, and people mistook him for Jones a few times, which he just loved.

As the years have gone by, the pain of my dad's absence has barely diminished. The biggest reason is probably because I have looked at life in the same way he did, and I've tried to spend as much time with my kids as he did with me. One of his most remarkable qualities was his balance when it came to living life. He was open to and interested in a variety of things, and he enjoyed life's adventure to the fullest.

Other than my wife, Barbara, I've never known anyone with a sounder set of values and a better sense of perspective on all facets of living than my father. He was the foundation on which I was able to become a world-class golfer, but not before he established the principles for trying to make me a better and more well-rounded person—and eventually spouse and father—who had the right set of priorities and didn't try to be bigger than the game. I think I've tried to display that through adhering to sportsmanship, and handling as best I could the other responsibilities that go with being part of a sport that is far greater than any one player.

It's in those capacities that I hope I have made him proudest.

JACK GROUT

JACK ARRIVED AT SCIOTO COUNTRY CLUB FROM TEXAS IN 1950, just when my father and I were taking our early tours of the course together. Jack asked my father if I would be interested in attending a junior program he was starting up. I quickly showed an aptitude for golf, and Jack Grout recognized in me some potential that he was only too happy to nurture. From the beginning the two of us just got along great together.

What's really important about the relationship Jack Grout and I shared is not that he taught me so many things—obviously, he did, and he established all the fundamentals, particularly key tenets such as keeping my head still throughout the swing, and that golf is played between the insides of the feet. What's important is that he showed interest in me and he spent time with

Jack Grout's junior golf class at Scioto in 1950. I'm third from the right.

me; he encouraged me and he was there for me, and that's like being another father. When your dad is there for you, you're part of an environment that makes you want to do things better, and that's the way Jack Grout was for me, especially after my own father's passing.

From the time I was eleven years old, Jack wouldn't accept a dime from my dad for the instruction he was giving me. At first I think it cost us forty-five bucks for the summer for the group lesson. A bucket of balls cost forty-five cents, and my dad would get the bill and say, "Hey,

Above: Jack corrects my mechanics. Right: I'll always treasure these words from Jack written the year before he passed away.

June 29, 1988

Dear Jack:

I appreciated your call more than I can tell you. As you might have guessed from my voice, I don't have a lot of pep these days. If I had had a little more energy, I would have told you a couple of things. Since I didn't or couldn't, I have asked Bonnie to write this letter.

This latest "Player of the Century" honor--for you to have placed ahead of Jones, Hogan, Nelson, Hagen, Snead and Sarazen, to mention a few I did know--was some kind of accomplishment. I think I know how you did it. I have decided that even greater than achievement in sport is high achievement in sportsmanship. Your Dad and your Mother taught you about that second one; and I think that's why you won.

Whether I taught you anything about golf or not, is not for me to say. If your development had stopped with your understanding of the mechanics of the game, Jack, it is possible that some of those other great players would have beat you out. What you have going for you, however, was born into you and then nurtured by your homelife. When Charlie told you you couldn't play anymore if you threw another club, he did you a favor, Jack.

You wouldn't be the "Player of the Century" if you weren't a heckuva player. They gave the honor to the guy who is a great sport and a great sportsman. As far as I am concerned you are the greatest golfer who ever swung a club in the history of the game.

I wish you the very best in the coming years. Needless to say I'd like to be thirty years younger, so I could share some more of the good times. All things considered, however, I don't think I have any reason to complain.

Sincerely,

Jack

Jack Grout

aren't we a little heavy on hitting golf balls?" He was more kidding than anything. But pretty soon I'd hit twenty buckets of balls and Jack would charge me for ten. Soon after that there wasn't a bill at all. Jack wanted to be part of my life, part of what I was doing, and part of watching me grow as a golfer and a person. That's the type of relationship we had.

Every year until Jack died in 1989, I would go back to him at the start of the season for a complete refresher course in the fundamentals. We'd go through things just like I was a beginner. As the season progressed I would go back to him for periodic checkups. One of his great talents, besides a keen eye for spotting flaws, was his economy of words. He never filled my head with long explanations. And whenever I asked a lot of technical, nitpicky questions, he was astute enough to evade them. He never fed me too much information or waxed philosophical about some method or theory. He imparted simple ideas and then let me try to master them my way.

Jack wanted to be part of my life, part of what I was doing, and part of watching me grow as a golfer and a person.

Could I have gotten along without Jack Grout teaching me how to play golf? Absolutely not. But one of Jack's greatest lessons was to teach me to one day be self-sufficient, to figure out my own game, be my own teacher, and to be able to correct myself on the golf course in critical situations in tournament play. That ability became my one of my most valuable assets. I eventually reached a point in my career when there might have been times I came to see Jack, but we'd talk about almost everything but golf. We weren't a teacher and a student, we were friends.

growing up in COLUMBUS

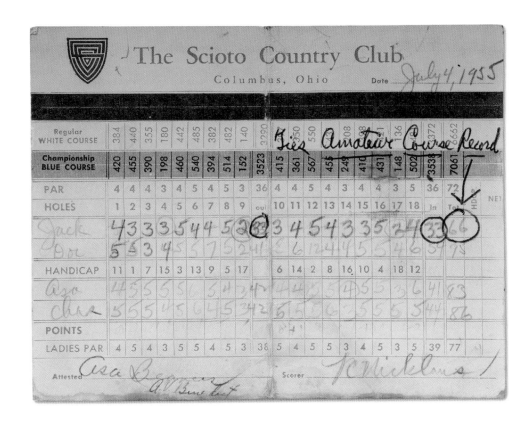

I TOOK PIANO LESSONS WHEN I WAS A KID. I didn't like them, not because I didn't have an appreciation for the musical arts, but simply because I didn't like being indoors. Also, there was no competition involved. I like competition.

I was in the Cub Scouts once. Didn't stick with that, either. The meetings were indoors. I was on the Safety Patrol in sixth grade. That was my speed. Outdoors.

Keeping up with me during my formative years in Columbus, Ohio, couldn't have been easy for my poor mom and dad. I was one busy kid, and that was without my increasing time on the golf course as I grew older and more proficient at the game. I think the following photos suffice

as proof that I wasn't consumed by golf growing up, though I've included a golf highlight as well: the scorecard from the course-record 66 I shot when I was fifteen years old.

But mixed in are your basic, everyday Americana photos and items. I was just your regular kid growing up in a loving family in the Midwest, with a passion for sports and games: there's the hayride with classmates when I was thirteen, and card games with my college fraternity brothers from Phi Gamma Delta when I was a student at Ohio State.

Despite tying the Scioto Country Club course record at fifteen (previous page), not all my time was spent on a golf course. There were also hayrides (left) and card games with fraternity brothers (above).

a WOODEN LAMP

MY BASKETBALL COACH, Mike Kish, was my industrial arts teacher, and I must have made this in about the eighth grade. This was one of the assignments that we had in school. I had to make a lamp on a lathe. You wouldn't know from this that I was good with my hands.

I'm not sure if I'd have made the cut as a woodworker, but at least this lamp from shop class is still in one piece.

BOB JONES

I NEVER SAW BOB JONES PLAY GOLF—not a single shot—but Mr. Jones, winner of the Grand Slam and founder of Augusta National Golf Club and the Masters Tournament, played a very special role in my life and in my golf career, and he also is a part of many of my favorite stories.

I first met Mr. Jones—I always called him Mr. Jones—when I qualified for my first national amateur. I was fifteen years old, and we were to compete on the James River Course at the Country Club of Virginia. I was walking off the eighteenth green of my final practice round (it was a long par-four of about 460 yards), and there was a gentleman in a cart sitting behind the green watching. It was Jones, and he called me over and said, "Young man, I've been sitting behind this green here for the last couple of hours, and you are one of only a few people to reach this green in two. I wanted to congratulate you."

Here I was, fifteen years old, playing in my first amateur, and Bob Jones was going to watch me play?

That night at the banquet Bob Jones was the speaker, and he stopped by my table and said, "Jack, I am going to come out tomorrow and watch you play a few holes." Here I was, fifteen years old, playing in my first amateur, and Bob Jones was going to watch me play?

I had to play Bob Gardner—who was a very good player who went on to play in the Walker Cup, World Cup, and many other international amateur events—in the first round, and I actually had Bob down after ten holes. But I kept looking around, over my shoulder, wondering, "Where's Bob Jones?" All of the sudden, coming down the tenth fairway, was Mr. Jones. He followed me for three holes—eleven, twelve, and thirteen—and I went bogey, bogey, double bogey. From 1-up

23

I fell to 2-down. He turned to my dad and said before leaving, "I don't think I am doing Jack any good out here." I got it back to an even score but lost the last hole. But what an experience, and what a great introduction to Bob Jones.

I had the pleasure of seeing Bob Jones many times after that. The most memorable, of course, was each time I went to Augusta for the Masters Tournament. Before my 1959 debut, he invited my father and me to his cabin. That became an annual event, sitting and talking to Mr. Jones for about a half hour, and it was a very special thing my father and I always looked forward to.

I had the privilege of speaking with Bob Jones many times. This picture was taken in Columbus, when I was 17.

Of course, I set my goals in golf based on the standards Bob Jones established in his career. He won thirteen major championships, and my goal was to see if I could come somewhere near that record. Soon after I turned professional, I made one of those bold and definitive comments I was prone to making, and said something to the effect of, "Jones is the greatest golfer who ever lived and probably ever will live. That's my goal: Bob Jones. It's the only goal." When I eventually surpassed it, the moment was as sad for me as it was sweet, because of what Bob Jones' record had meant to my life and the place it had held in golf history.

I set my goals in golf based on the standards Bob Jones established in his career.

I don't think I've admired any athlete more than I admired Bob Jones. He embodied everything that is so special about golf, particularly amateur golf. To win the British Amateur, British Open, U.S. Open, and U.S. Amateur in one year took remarkable playing skills, in addition to the resourcefulness to remain amateur. Whether he was the greatest golfer in history may be debated for years with no definitive conclusion, but without argument, he was the greatest golfer of his time, as special as there ever was.

the DECISION *to turn* PRO

IN TODAY'S SPORTS CLIMATE, there really isn't any debate at all about whether or not a player should turn professional. If he or she is good enough, the only question for that player is when. I don't have an opinion about whether this player or that player is ready to play professionally. They should have determination, and the maturity to handle the pressure and the distractions, but each individual has to decide when he is ready.

When I confronted the question of remaining an amateur or turning professional in 1961, the decision was far more complicated and difficult than it is now. I knew in my heart that I wanted to be the best golfer that I could, but I also knew that my parents hoped I would remain an amateur and that I would pursue golf in the same manner as my dad's idol, Bob Jones, had done. I was well aware of Jones' record, too, and I couldn't become the "next Jones" if I turned pro. The thought of the countless hours of travel and time away from home as a Tour player wasn't very appealing to me, either, and at the time I also was trying to finish up my degree at Ohio State. On top of that, the issue of wanting to defend my second U.S. Amateur title weighed against the nagging thought that maybe I had accomplished all I wanted to as an amateur.

There was plenty on my plate.

While I was mulling over the question, Jones, of all people, weighed in himself, and wrote me a nice letter encouraging me to remain an amateur. But he said he would fully understand my decision if I turned pro. He added something like, "And if you do turn professional, I've been involved with Spalding for quite a while, and you should talk to them. I could arrange an introduction."

This picture is from the 1961 Masters, seven months before I turned pro.

Money was certainly a factor in professional sports at the time I was trying to decide whether or not to turn professional, but it wasn't nearly as influential as it is today. I wanted to do what I thought was best—not only for me, but also for Barbara and little Jack—but money wasn't really a part of the equation. Even at twenty-one, I was smart enough to know you couldn't use money as a motivator. Besides, I already was earning enough to make a decent living, and playing professional golf seemed to come with more risks and less security. I'd guess I was making $24,000 a year at the time, which was pretty good for a kid in those days. I made $12,000 selling insurance, $6,000 working for a slacks company and $6,000 more playing golf for the slacks manufacturer. Heck, my first house cost only $22,000. Had I kept on at those things, I'd have done fine, but I would have been miserable. All I ever wanted to do was play competitive golf against the best players in the world.

I could have continued playing top amateur tournaments, but that wasn't going to keep me interested.

So my decision to turn pro was based on wanting to be the best golfer I could be, playing against the best competition, and that was the only way to do it. That's the only way you *could* do it. Sure, I could have continued playing top amateur tournaments, but that wasn't going to keep me interested, and playing golf recreationally wasn't going to be much of a test, either.

Finally I made the decision and announced my intentions to be a pro golfer on November 8, 1961, but only after writing a letter to Joe Dey, the head of the United States Golf Association, and then again phoning him so that he was fully aware of what I was going to do. That letter wasn't the easiest one to write, but Barbara and my dad, reluctant as he was to see me give up my amateur status, helped me with it, and like everything else I did, I never looked back. I never wondered if I made the right choice. I just put my head down, went full speed ahead, and tried to find out just how high I could climb up that mountain.

WOODY HAYES

I WAS FORTUNATE TO HAVE A TREMENDOUS SUPPORT NETWORK AROUND ME GROWING UP IN COLUMBUS, and this was a comforting circumstance as I became more involved in golf and started competing away from home. This included more than my mother, father, and Jack Grout. There was a group of regulars who never hesitated to hit the road and keep my dad company outside the ropes while I played.

Woody Hayes was a great friend to our family, and one of the most compassionate people I've ever known. This picture is from the 1976 Memorial Tournament.

One of my biggest supporters was Woody Hayes, the legendary Ohio State University football coach, who lived a block and a half from my dad's pharmacy on campus, and became a close friend to both my dad and me. Woody knew I played several sports, and that I especially loved football. I was a quarterback, linebacker, and placekicker in junior high. I dreamed of playing football at Ohio State. My dad, who played some professional football, once asked Woody for advice about me and my future in football. Woody said, "Football is a great game, but I know the talents of your son in golf. Keep him as far away from my game as you can." He didn't say I couldn't make the team at Ohio State. He merely implied that golf was my best game and that I should focus on that. So I stuck with golf and basketball the remainder of high school.

Woody attended many of my tournaments. He was on hand when I won the 1959 U.S. Amateur Championship at The Broadmoor in Colorado Springs, Colorado, and even phoned back to the Columbus newspapers with results of my matches. At the 1962 U.S. Open, he was part of the group that followed me around the golf course at Oakmont Country Club, near Pittsburgh, and it was probably a good thing he was there. Although I was oblivious to the negative comments from some members of the gallery who were pulling so hard for their hometown favorite, Arnold Palmer, my father heard plenty, and he didn't appreciate the things people were saying about his son. It was Woody who kept him calm.

Here's the type of person Woody was: When Barbara's mother died, Woody came by the funeral home. The atmosphere was sad, but at one point I looked over, and there was Woody in a corner with my four boys—he was giving them a lesson on military history, deflecting the sadness as best he could. I was thinking how thoughtful that was when Barbara got a phone call. It was Woody's wife, wanting to know if Woody was there. She asked if he had his walker with him, and whether his car was in the parking lot. It turned out Woody had just had a stroke and wasn't supposed to be out of the house, let alone not have his walker. He certainly shouldn't have been trying to drive a car. But he wanted to be there for Barbara and the boys, and he had snuck out of the house.

Woody touched many lives, including ours. Anyone who knew him would share my opinion that he was a very special person and a great man.

1959: *my* FIRST TRIP *to* SCOTLAND

The Captain and Members of
The Royal and Ancient Golf Club of St. Andrews
request the pleasure of the company of
Mr. J. W. Nicklaus.
at a Walker Cup Dinner on Saturday 16th May 1959.
in The Marine Hotel, North Berwick.

8 p.m. for 8.30 pm.
Dress:- Lounge suits.

R.S.V.P. to The Secretary.
Royal and Ancient Golf Club,
St. Andrews.

OF ALL THE LANDS IN WHICH I HAVE BEEN FORTUNATE TO PLAY GOLF, Scotland is my favorite, ever since I made my first trip there in May 1959, a trip that probably had as much to do with the course I would take in my life as any experience I'd had in the game up to that point.

I was nineteen years old when I got my first taste of golf abroad. I'd been selected to play for the United States in that year's Walker Cup matches, a biennial competition between amateur players from the United States and players from Great Britain and Ireland. Aside from the great honor this was to play for my country, and the fact that a Walker Cup berth at the time resulted in an invitation to play in the Masters Tournament, being selected for the Walker Cup made me realize I was a fairly decent golfer. Having a chance to go to Scotland was a big deal. It gave me an opportunity to test myself in another environment. I had a chance to play all those old links courses, which are so different from what we play here at home. And although I played well in the Walker Cup, I found out that I still had a lot of growing to do as a player.

It was a great honor to be named to the U.S. Walker Cup team in 1959, prior to the competition.

Going to the United Kingdom meant I wasn't going to be able to play for the Ohio State golf team that spring, and I was apprehensive about telling my coach, Bob Kepler. But Kep couldn't have been nicer or more supportive. I said, "Kep, I made the Walker Cup team. That might put a crimp in our spring plans of playing golf." And he said, "Don't be silly, you're going to play in the

My mother and I were surprised by the sendoff I received at the Columbus airport before boarding the plane for Scotland.

British Amateur, and the Walker Cup matches, and you're going to be a golfer. Don't worry about the golf team, we'll be fine. This is fantastic; this is great for you." That's the golf coach I had, and that's the kind of golf team we had at Ohio State.

While I was playing the matches at Muirfield, the oldest golf club in the world, and home to the Honourable Company of Edinburgh Golfers, my dad took the opportunity to go play the Old Course at Royal & Ancient Golf Club of St. Andrews, which isn't far away. He and three friends played, and when he came back I asked him, "How did you enjoy St. Andrews?" He said, "What an awful golf course. There are bumps all over the place." Of course, he's an American, and he had never played anything like it, and later I found out that he had three-putted fifteen times on those large, bumpy greens.

Me, I loved links golf right away. I loved the challenges. Muirfield was just fascinating to me, and it would end up influencing my golf life significantly. Seven years later at Muirfield, at the 1966 British Open, with the course set up in a way that was not a good fit for my golf game—high rough lining narrow fairways—I managed my game and my nerves about as well as I ever have, and won my first Open Championship to complete the career Grand Slam. And later when it came time to conceive a name for the golf club I was building in suburban Columbus in the early 1970s, Muirfield came to mind again, and Muirfield Village Golf Club was born. The club logo has a silhouette of the Claret Jug, the trophy presented to that year's Champion Golfer, the title bestowed upon the man who wins the British Open.

Prior to the Walker Cup, I played at Royal St. George's, in Sandwich, England, in the Grand Challenge Cup, which I won. Afterward, I competed in my only British Amateur championship, also at St. Andrews. I lost in the quarterfinals to Bill Hyndman. But win or lose, I enjoyed the experience immensely, and that's when my love affair with Scottish golf and the people of Scotland began, and when golf really became a focus to me. Not long after that I won the U.S. Amateur Championship for my first national title. The die was cast, as they say.

BEN HOGAN

WE HONORED BEN HOGAN AT THE MEMORIAL TOURNAMENT IN 1999, and it was long overdue, not only for the game of golf, but for me, personally. He would have been our choice to be honoree many years before that, but Ben didn't want to be honored while he was alive. So when he passed away the year before, it was time we gave him his due, and that meant a great deal to me because I probably had as good a relationship with Ben as any of the older champions, though obviously I liked them all and had great respect for them.

I was lucky enough to play in an exhibition with Sam Snead when I was fifteen years old. After that Sam always called me Junior. When I got into my thirties and forties and he still called me Junior, which I thought was kind of a neat thing between the two of us. Sam always had a great sense of humor, but he also cleared out a few Champions Dinners at the Masters with his jokes. He was a character and a real piece of work. I've always said his was among the greatest swings and certainly the most fluid motion in the game of golf.

Hogan, in my mind, was the best ball-striker I've ever seen, meticulous in his course management and his strategy.

Hogan, it's fair to say, was the complete opposite: a very reserved and private man. And while Snead might have had the most graceful swing, Hogan, in my mind, was the best ball-striker I've ever seen, meticulous in his course management and his strategy.

My own relationship with Hogan, who was a friend of my teacher Jack Grout, goes back to the 1960 U.S. Open. The first time I met him, we were paired for the last two rounds at Cherry Hills, back when we played thirty-six holes on Saturday to complete the tournament. He was

great to play with. He was as courteous as he could be, but he didn't say a lot, just occasionally, when he wanted to. He wasn't a whole lot different than I was. I don't like to talk a whole lot, or listen to a bunch of chatter, either. I like to play golf—particularly when I'm playing something I want to play well in. I don't want to talk about what kind of birds are in the trees or something. Maybe that's why we got along so well.

The record shows that I finished second to Arnold in that Open, but Hogan might well have won it for the way he struck the ball. His chances ended when he left a wedge approach short and ended up in the water in front of the seventeenth green in the final round. Up until then he had hit all thirty-four greens in regulation, not to mention all eighteen in the previous round. But that was at the time when he was starting to stand over a putt much longer than he did during

The first time I met Ben Hogan, we were paired together at the 1960 U.S. Open.

his prime. He missed a fair number of short putts that day, though he did hole some longer putts. But I remember the shot-making display he put on that day was just fantastic.

As with Snead, watching Hogan's swing sort of stuck with me, and I played like Hogan, or thought I did, for most of the rest of that summer, trying to take my left side and keep it ahead of my right and never let it catch up. To me, Hogan looked like he played that way, and I tried to imitate that; kids do those kinds of things. He was always an inspiration to me every time I watched him hit golf balls.

I never got tired of watching Hogan play or even just practice, and it was always flattering when he asked me to join him.

The next year at the Masters, Hogan was one of the first guys I saw when I walked into the clubhouse. He says, "Hey, Fella, want to play?" (Just as Sam always called me "Junior," Hogan called everybody "Fella.") I said, "Fine. Let's go." Same thing at the U.S. Open at Oakland Hills later in the summer. I enjoyed watching him, and since I didn't like to talk, he must have felt like I was good company, I guess. From then on we played a reasonable amount of golf together, and I never got tired of watching Hogan play or even just practice, and it was always flattering when he asked me to join him.

Hogan and I never talked about this—I really don't know if he even remembered—but he wrote a letter to me quite a few years before we played together in that U.S. Open at Cherry Hills. Here's a copy of that letter, which I received about a month before my seventeenth birthday. For a kid my age, it was quite a thrill.

You don't realize the significance of some of the things you accomplish until you receive a wonderful letter such as this.

December 14, 1956

MR. JACK NICKLAUS
2074 Collingswood Avenue
Columbus, Ohio

Dear Jack:

Recently your outstanding golf record was brought to my
attention, and I would like to take this opportunity to congratulate you on all your fine achievements!

I also understand that you started playing golf when you
were ten years old and have taken lessons since that
time under tutelage of Jack Grout, who happens to be a
life long friend of mine.

I do not know the name brand of the equipment you play,
but if you are not already playing the Ben Hogan Clubs,
I would consider it a personal favor if you would give
them just ONE try!

Meanwhile, wishing you continued success, and with
kindest personal regards, I am

Sincerely

Ben

VIA AIRMAIL

1962: *my* FIRST PAYCHECK

I RECEIVED A FAIR AMOUNT OF PRESS COVERAGE WHEN I COMPETED IN MY FIRST PRO-
FESSIONAL TOURNAMENT, the Los Angeles Open, in early January 1962. It was flattering that
some writers thought I might "win everything" when I got on the Tour. I had some expectations
for myself, but of course there was also plenty of anxiety. My start as a professional didn't necessarily relieve me of any doubts.

Of course, one of the realities of Tour life back then was that you didn't have much of a choice
but to do well, or you weren't going to be around very long—and even then the money wasn't
such that you could make a living strictly playing golf, not like you can today. When I played my
first year on the Tour, I think the average purse was around $35,000 or so. We played about eight
to ten tournaments of $20,000, nine of them were $50,000, and only one of them was more than
that—the Thunderbird was the first $100,000 tournament with a $20,000 first prize.

My first tournament check as a professional was worth $33.33—a one-third share of last place at the Los Angeles Open.

As it turned out, it took me awhile to get to those upper pay scales. All that press coverage before the L.A. Open was equaled by the same amount of attention afterward, when the reigning U.S. Amateur champ put together some unimpressive scores of 74-70-72-73-289. That placed me in a tie for fiftieth, twenty-one shots behind the winner, my good friend Phil Rodgers. For that I earned my first official prize winnings: $33.33, which represented one-third of last-place money. At least I made the cut.

(A little piece of trivia: my first actual check as a professional was $75, for a speech I made to the White-Haines Optical Company in Columbus in late 1961.)

Eventually, I won three tournaments my first year, plus the World Series of Golf, and the money was all right for the times. I won $17,500 when I won the U.S. Open, $2,800 when I won in Portland, and another $2,800 when I won in Seattle. I finished third on the money list behind Arnold Palmer and Gene Littler, with almost $62,000. Looking back you can see just how much the game has changed from the prize money standpoint.

At last year's Memorial Tournament, the total purse was $5.5 million. My career earnings are a little more than $5.7 million.

When a guy wins a regular tour event today, he wins almost a million dollars. He almost doesn't need to bother with the rest of the year. Guys get their pockets filled earlier, but then again, it's probably harder to win today. It's a worldwide game. There are an awful lot of players who come out, and golf is their business and their livelihood, and that's the way they go after it. At last year's Memorial Tournament, the total purse was $5.5 million. My career earnings are a little more than $5.7 million. Like I said, it's a different era. I never played the game for money; I played the game for the game, for the competition, and for the trophies. I just figured money would come if I played the game well. Maybe that's part of the reason why I like the era in which I played.

I may not have done all that well in my first tournament, but that little check has an enormous amount of meaning for me. It represents the beginning of a pretty neat journey.

my MACGREGOR 3-WOOD

SOME GOLF CLUBS YOU JUST CAN'T BEAR TO PART WITH. I had one club that I carried with me for all twenty of my major championship victories—a Tommy Armour 3-wood manufactured by MacGregor. I started using it when I was eighteen years old, and it was a great club. Back then, when you found a club you could use, you didn't fiddle around with it, you just went ahead and used it.

It was standard length; it was counterbalanced. I think it actually had my name on it, too. It had sort of a wing-shaped plate on it, and I think that's where my name was, and it was big enough that you could almost read it. What's funny is that from 1958 to 1983 I never changed the grip. It was made of leather, and after a period of time leather grips tended to get a little slick. Though I got a new set of irons just about every year, I never changed that 3-wood. So, I had a slick grip on the 3-wood and the other ones had a reasonable tackiness to them, which didn't make any sense, but like I said, it worked for me and I just went with that. When I did finally decide to change the grip, the club never really seemed the same to me after that. Go figure.

I had a lot of work done to the head of the club through the years so I could keep it in play. It cracked a couple of times, and I would always get it repaired because it was so reliable. There's no telling how many golf balls I hit with it over those twenty-five years of tournament golf.

I wasn't as lucky with other clubs. For instance, in my last year as an amateur, I tried a bunch of drivers made by MacGregor. I think they made me fourteen drivers that year, and I broke the faces out of about ten of them. But one of those drivers was the one that I finally ended up settling

on, and I used that from 1961 through 1966, until it broke in two pieces in South Africa when I was playing in a tournament with Gary Player. The head just exploded. That hurt. In those days you couldn't walk out to the pro shop on the golf course where the pros are, have them make up fifty drivers for you, and figure out which one you want to use. If you found one, you hung onto it as long as possible.

The 3-wood was never the same after I had the grip changed, but I did squeeze one more major out of it: the 1986 Masters. On the eighteenth hole of the final round at Augusta National, when I really needed to hit that fairway and make at the very least a par to finish off my round, what did I grab? You bet. I hit the 3-wood, and it didn't let me down.

I started using this particular MacGregor 3-wood (left) when I was eighteen. Here I am in the 1978 U.S. Open (above).

experimenting with PUTTERS

I'VE NEVER BELIEVED THAT WHEN IT COMES TO PUTTING, the implement is as important as the person wielding it. Most of my best streaks with the putter were usually the product of inspiration more than anything. I was fortunate that my powers of concentration were such that when the heat was really on, I didn't miss many putts, although everybody is going to miss their share. But anybody who is a champion doesn't miss many putts under pressure, and there's no escaping the fact that putting, which Ben Hogan called a game within the game, often can weigh disproportionately on the outcome of a round.

I have to admit that through the years I benefited from some timely putting tips that carried me to some of my most important victories. Jack Grout had a keen eye for spotting flaws, but I also received advice from Jackie Burke, Deane Beman, Bruce Devlin, and my son, Jackie. Whether my backswing was too long or I was dragging the putter through the ball or I was breaking off my stroke, I had my flaws and occasionally someone came to my rescue. It was Jackie Burke, in fact, who offered a tip on my technique during a practice round in Palm Springs in 1962 that became a key fundamental I've never stopped using. Always a fine putter, Burke thought I was pulling the putter head through the ball and suggested that I set my right thumb on top of the shaft and my palm underneath it and then use my right hand to push the putter

through the ball. I felt better about my putting almost immediately.

Tips aside, there were occasions, as we all find, when I found a bit of magic in a new club.

That happened more than once, including early in my career. George Low, whose reputation as a fine putter was unquestioned, offered to let me try one of his new clubs at the '62 Phoenix Open. It was a flanged-blade model called the "Wizard 600." The putter was two ounces heavier than the Ben Sayers, wooden-shafted model I had made for me in North Berwick, Scotland, during the '59 Walker Cup matches, which I'd been using since. That doesn't seem like much of a difference, but the first time I used the Wizard 600, I shot 64 in the Pro-Am, and I have no doubt that putter contributed more to my overall record than any single club today, except for maybe the MacGregor 3-wood.

The Wizard 600 might have been the most important putter I ever wielded, but it was far from the most familiar. Two other models I used sparingly, but during key victories, have assumed a lofty status in golf lore. The first of these is a center-shafted Bull's Eye putter that came to be known as White Fang, which Fred Mueller, a friend of Deane Beman's, gave to me just before I won the 1967

I've used a number of memorable putters over the years. Opposite: A replica of the Response ZT (left), White Fang, and the Wizard 600. Above: The Ben Sayers model I had made for me in Scotland in 1959.

U.S. Open at Baltusrol. The brass head of the putter was painted white to dull the sun's glare. Deane helped me adjust the grip, sticking a pencil in the back of it, breaking it off, and then wrapping it up. In combination with another putting tip, this one from an Ohio pal and good player, Gordon Jones, I putted quite well on some very difficult greens, and collected my second Open title, punctuated by a closing 65 and a 275 total, which eclipsed Ben Hogan's championship record by one stroke.

Fast-forward almost twenty years now, to 1986 and the Masters Tournament. I hadn't won a major in six years, but through hard work and my own bullheaded determination I was able to elevate my ball-striking. Now if I could only get my putter to work, which is essential to success at Augusta. For much of the spring I had been using a new model manufactured by MacGregor. I first saw the putter in the summer of 1985 and thought it was a joke. I had asked Clay Long, the head of research and development for MacGregor and who now works at Nicklaus Golf Equipment,

I hadn't won a major in six years, but through hard work and my own bullheaded determination I was able to elevate my ball-striking.

to make a putter similar to the Ping Pal that Tom Watson was using. Instead, he gave me this contraption that, with a few tweaks, became a high-inertia putter. After experimenting with it a little, I found that I could get the ball rolling nicely. I put the Response ZT in my bag when the PGA Tour got to the Florida Swing.

I was at the TPC at Eagle Trace in Coral Springs, Florida, for the Honda Classic, when I began to question whether or not using it was a good idea. The club was so big that the wind would affect it. I remember having a six-inch putt at Eagle Trace, where the wind blows pretty hard, and a gust came up and nudged that light putter head, and I stubbed the putter on the turf and left the putt short. I thought, "Oh, man, what have I got this thing in my hands for?" And I think the public looked at it and thought the same thing, because we didn't sell many up to that point.

The Response ZT putter was a big part of my 1986 Masters victory.

We couldn't give it away prior to the Masters. But I stayed with it because once I got used to the lightness of the putter, I could make the ball roll nicely. I used that putter until 1988, and why I stopped I don't have any idea. If I were still playing I might think about using that model again. After I won the Masters, we couldn't make that putter fast enough. I think we sold maybe 20,000 of them before the Masters, and eventually sold about 350,000 of them after I won.

There is a postscript to share about White Fang and the Response ZT.

Much to my disappointment, both of my clubs had gone AWOL by the time the museum opened. I didn't have a clue what had happened to them. Then in 2003, I received a gift out of the blue, even though it was my son, Steve, who was celebrating a birthday—his fortieth, in fact. Joe Wessel, who played defensive back for Florida State University and was one of Steve's roommates, came up to me at the party with a club in his hand. He said, "Mr. Nicklaus, I found this club in my garage. Does it have any significance?" I recognized it instantly: it was White Fang. The way you could tell was not the white head but at the grip where the pencil had been shoved in and broken off all those years ago. Steve had let Joe borrow it at some point. I smiled and said, "Joe, that's one of only two clubs that I'm missing from my major-championship days." He asked me

I stayed with it because once I got used to the lightness of the putter, I could make the ball roll nicely.

if I wanted it, and I had to tell him that, of course, but that it was worth a lot of money. Joe said simply, "Take my dad to Augusta for a round of golf and we're even."

That brings me to the Response ZT, now the only club, as of this writing, that I haven't found. Like my old Bull's Eye, it's now probably in a garage somewhere. Several copies of the club have turned up, but not the original. Someday maybe somebody will look in his garage or clean out his attic, find a putter, one that's lightweight and has a big head, and wonder if it's worth anything.

It is to me—sentimentally, at least.

BARBARA

MY LIFE HAS NEVER BEEN THE SAME SINCE THE FIRST WEEK OF MY FRESHMAN YEAR AT OHIO STATE UNIVERSITY IN SEPTEMBER 1957, and I thank God for that every day. That was the week I met a tall, slim, beautiful, and sweet girl named Barbara Bash. It didn't take me long to figure out that our chance meeting, on the steps of Menden Hall on the OSU campus, was a stroke of good fortune; I called her up later that evening and asked her out for a date.

We were both seventeen at the time, just kids, and I think we clicked because we shared similar values and priorities, like the importance of family. All these years later, with all the good things that have happened to me, I still believe that Barbara has been the most precious gift in my life. We were married in 1960, and we have grown up together, really. She has been my foundation, my voice of reason, my sounding board, my biggest supporter, my best friend, and the love of my life.

In 1998, the PGA of America gave Barbara a well-deserved First Lady of Golf award.

The impact she's had on me, both personally and professionally, is truly too big to fully measure or adequately explain. Barbara had never played golf or been around the game when we met, but it wasn't long before she could hold her own with anyone on the subject of the game. I imagine she has walked more golf courses than anyone on Tour except the players, and she may have many of them beaten, too. In fact, you could do worse than follow her around, because she always has the shortest routes and best vantage points mapped out.

Barbara had never played golf or been around the game when we met, but it wasn't long before she could hold her own with anyone on the subject of the game.

While I was planning and building Muirfield Village Golf Club, I had a lot of help and support, but Barbara was unswerving in her belief in what I was trying to accomplish, and she threw herself into the project as enthusiastically as I did. In effect, my dreams became her dreams. The most selfless person I've ever known, Barbara assimilated her life to fit what I was trying to achieve in the game, even at the beginning when she didn't understand golf and its nuances as well as she does now. The daughter of a schoolteacher who arrived home after work at almost the same time every day, Barbara had to get used to the unpredictable hours that a golf professional keeps, in addition to all the other challenges that go with Tour life.

Barbara's support over the years allowed me to concentrate on the things I needed to do to be successful in a difficult line of work, and I think you'll find that many of the game's best players enjoyed the same kind of support at home. Without her I might have become just another golfer. It's not only her devotion to me and my career that has been important. Her organizational skills and her sense of priorities always eased my mind when I was on the road; I never had to worry about how the kids were doing or any other problem that might arise, because she handled everything

Me and the love of my life, captured in 1966 at Augusta National Golf Club in Augusta, Georgia.

so well. Because of her patience, love, and support, combined with her intelligence and strength of character, Barbara has been a bigger contributor to my golf career than the world will ever know. We have some wonderful pictures of the two of us holding up trophies, and I think those are the most appropriate we have, because we've really achieved victories as a team.

As such, Barb also had a way of appealing to my better nature and smoothing some of my rough edges. I've never had much trouble saying no to people, only because if I didn't learn to budget my time properly, I'd have never gotten anything done. Barbara is just the opposite: She can't say no to anyone, and she's probably the best listener in the world, always willing to help friends or acquaintances with problems big or small.

Barbara's immense capacity for caring and putting others ahead of herself is evidenced by the many charitable causes she supports. For years, the Children's Hospital in Columbus, Ohio, has been a passion of hers, and more recently, she's poured herself into the Nicklaus Children's Health Care Foundation and the Nicklaus Children's Hospital at St. Mary's Medical Center in West Palm Beach, Florida.

If your partner in life is also your best friend, it's truly invaluable. I shudder to think about where I would be today, what I might have missed, how less fulfilling my life would have been were Barbara not with me every step of the way.

Barbara and Michael helped me take home the Wanamaker Trophy after I won the 1980 PGA Championship.

JULY 23, 1960: *our* WEDDING DAY

I NEVER LOST A LONG-DRIVE CONTEST AS A PROFESSIONAL, and they had quite a few on the Tour in the early days of my career. But I did lose one to my friends on my last hole as a single man.

Barb and I agreed on July 23 for what I thought was an excellent reason: It coincided with that year's PGA Championship.

It was July 23, 1960, and it was a hot, humid, typical Ohio summer day—the day Barbara and I chose for our wedding day. The ceremony was scheduled for 7:30 that evening, followed by a reception in the Scioto Country Club clubhouse. Barb and I agreed on July 23 for what I thought

This hand-painted gift plate was one of the special and personal gifts Barb and I received on our wedding day.

was an excellent reason: It coincided with that year's PGA Championship, which happened to be up the road at a golf course I grew to enjoy immensely—the South Course at Firestone Country Club in Akron, Ohio, where I made my debut in a Tour event in the 1958 Rubber City Open, and where I eventually won several tournaments, including the 1975 PGA. Still an amateur golfer at the time, I wasn't eligible to compete in the year's final major. Now for a confession: With such

Barbara looked absolutely beautiful, as usual, at our wedding. I tried not to look as nervous as I felt. At right: Our wedding invitation.

a big step coming up in my life, I didn't give golf much thought after the U.S. Open the month prior, where I lost to Arnold Palmer at Cherry Hills.

The day Barb and I tied the knot is one of the most cherished of my life, but before I get to that, there was one low point—how I finished up my round of golf the day before at Scioto. When I stepped up to the tee at the par-four home hole, I told my playing partners to stand way back because, this being my last drive as a single man, I was going to really wallop one. Well, I reared back and practically exploded out of my shoes trying to hit that ball. I really launched myself into that ball. But all I did was nick the top of it and it dribbled off the tee. The howls of laughter still ring in my ears as we watched the ball roll into a creek about twenty yards in front of me.

The following day went much more smoothly, though as one might expect, I was definitely nervous. Barbara looked beautiful as always. I did my best to measure up. I can recall that the reception was a lot of fun—and, boy, did we have a great time. As I mentioned before, it was hot, and we must have had more than three hundred guests there, so we stood in the reception line for quite a while greeting folks. Behind the reception line, the caterer kept filling glasses of champagne punch, and although for most of my adult life, I have never been much on drinking alcohol, that night I ended up enjoying my share of it. When the reception ended, we got in the car and Barbara drove us to a hotel across town, where I had checked us in as Mr. and Mrs. Smith, which fooled no one.

I was out like a light as soon as my head hit the pillow.

Mr. and Mrs. Stanley Stephens Bash
request the honour of your presence
at the marriage of their daughter
Barbara Jean
to
Mr. Jack William Nicklaus
on Saturday, the twenty-third of July
Nineteen hundred and sixty
at half after seven o'clock
North Broadway Methodist Church
Columbus, Ohio

1961: U.S. AMATEUR

I FELL IN LOVE WITH PEBBLE BEACH GOLF LINKS THE MOMENT I STEPPED FOOT ON THAT GORGEOUS PUBLIC COURSE, in preparation for the 1961 U.S. Amateur. I have said many times that if I had one more round to play in my life, it would be at Pebble Beach. It's no wonder I've enjoyed great success there over the years, including the '72 U.S. Open.

Winning my second national amateur title at Pebble is another highlight, and it was as pleasing as the first triumph two years earlier (though the '59 Amateur was more significant from the standpoint of establishing my credentials on a national level and setting up my future). The '61 Amateur, though, might well have been, start to finish, one of my most thoroughly solid performances in a major championship.

I have said many times that if I had one more round to play in my life, it would be at Pebble Beach.

There was no question my form was quite good that week, which culminated with an 8-and-6 victory over Dudley Wysong in the final. The scorecards reveal that over eight matches, I was a combined twenty under par for the 112 holes. I shot under par in every match and lost only nineteen holes.

The inspiration I drew from Pebble Beach and my sound form put me in a good frame of mind for the championship, but further easing any worries was the addition of a pre-tournament routine that ended up serving me well throughout my career.

Up until my arrival at Pebble Beach, I played golf like everyone before me, estimating distances on approach shots to greens, or shots where you lay up short of a bunker or hazard. They didn't have

yardages on sprinkler heads back then, let alone laser range finders. This added another layer to the challenge of managing your game, and I was always decent at judging distances, but not exceptional. While playing a practice round with my Walker Cup teammate Deane Beman, I told him about my troubles, especially with the blustery winds coming in off the Pacific Ocean. "Why don't you pace off the yardages then?" he said. Beman, as ever, made perfect sense. The extra information

Runner-up Dudley Wysong and I manage to kill time at Pebble Beach as the early morning mist clears.

could only help, and it fit perfectly with the way I liked to go around a golf course.

I went out the next day with a scorecard and marched off distances to the greens from prominent landmarks. For instance, at the first hole, I played off the left bunker and from there I had 138 yards to the front of the green, 162 to the back. At other holes I would use trees or bushes. Bing Crosby, who hosted the old Crosby Clambake for many years before it became the AT&T Pebble Beach Pro-Am, had a home off the thirteenth hole, which ran parallel to the ninth hole. I always used two trees in Bing Crosby's yard near his bay window as a marker, and the distance to the front of the ninth green from there was 187 yards. At the thirteenth, those trees were 113 yards from the front edge.

I always used two trees in Bing Crosby's yard near his bay window as a marker.

I kept that scorecard for years until the writing practically wore off, and then I transferred it to another card. In fact, until the last few years of my regular tour career, I kept every annotated scorecard from every tournament course I played.

I took home some beautiful hardware from the 1961 U.S. Amateur, which I consider to be one of my finest performances in a major championship.

my MUSICAL TASTES

AS EVERYONE WELL KNOWS, there is no use trying to get rid of a song that's stuck in your head, but sometimes that's not such a bad thing if you're on the golf course. If there is a song in your head when you get to the first tee, you can only hope it's a good one. I've played very well to Harry Belafonte singing "Jamaica Farewell." And it's hard to play badly to "Raindrops Keep Falling on My Head."

My musical tastes, if I were to try and classify them, probably tilt toward what might be called easy listening. For instance, Barb and I like Celine Dion among artists today. I guess growing up my preferences were pretty standard with the times. Rock 'n' roll came along, of course, and I enjoyed some of that. I liked the Four Freshmen and the Four Lads. Jackie Gleason's "For Lovers Only" was popular, and I was always a big fan of Frank Sinatra and Doris Day.

Then along came the Beatles, and here is where I diverged from my peers. When they came on the scene, I thought their music was so far out there. I thought they were pretty wild at the time, but now I really enjoy the Beatles. I can listen to songs like "Yesterday," and I just love that now, it's a great song.

I've gotten to be friends with some performers over the years. One was Billy Maxted, who toured with his Manhattan Jazz Band, and often performed in Columbus at the Grandview Inn. Barbara and I enjoyed his music and we became friends with Billy and his wife, Inez. Billy was very talented, and he had a big hit with Duke Ellington's "Satin Doll."

At some point he wrote a song called "The Golden Bear," and he asked me to do a cover shot with him. I didn't get a chance to do that, but he put out a record, *Billy Maxted Salutes "The Golden Bear."* I was asked not long ago if the song is any good. Honestly, I wouldn't know what it sounds like. I've only heard it a couple of times, and that was quite a few years ago. If you have

a record player, then you can hear it. I doubt there are many copies of the album out there.

Then there's Don Cherry, the crooner, who not only is a terrific performer, but also was a very good golfer and a good friend. He was a teammate of mine on the 1961 Walker Cup team in Seattle, and in the America's Cup Matches. Don finished fourth in the U.S. Open in 1960 at Cherry Hills. We both broke the Open record for an amateur player. He eventually turned professional, and he did pretty well.

Cherry is what you would call a singer's singer. Before a new song was cut by Dean Martin or Frank Sinatra or any of those guys, they would often have Cherry sing it first to see how it should be sung. He did everything from "Band of Gold," which was a pretty big hit, to the jingle for Mr. Clean, which he wrote for the Procter & Gamble Company in the 1950s. I've got tons of his records at home now. I've got a CD I play every day on the airplane with Cherry and Willie Nelson singing together. The name of the CD is "Augusta." Don, of course, played in several Masters Tournaments. He still sings great at age eighty-one.

I remember he was in Columbus once for a performance, and we had him over to the house on Elmwood Avenue for Thanksgiving dinner. Something happened to the biscuits; they weren't baked through. Cherry took one of the biscuits and threw it against the wall, and it stuck to the wall. I laughed, but I don't think my wife or mother did.

Don Cherry was every bit as accomplished swinging a golf club as he was singing into a microphone.

the origin of "GOLDEN BEAR"

I WAS A GOLDEN BEAR LONG BEFORE I WAS REFERRED TO AS THE GOLDEN BEAR.

I've seen it written a time or two that the inspiration for my nickname came from my youth. I attended Upper Arlington High School, where our nickname was the Golden Bears, but this is just a happy coincidence. To find the real source of how I eventually became known as the Golden Bear, you have to travel to Australia.

Now, I had plenty of nicknames in college, but "Blobbo" wasn't going to work as a suitable logo to put on a shirt, and I needed one for a new line of sports shirts and sweaters that I was going

I wore the Golden Bear logo for the 2005 Masters.

to be endorsing shortly after I turned professional. Then one day I recalled a story that appeared in the *Melbourne Age* a few months earlier. The writer, Don Lawrence, had interviewed Mark McCormack, the founder of International Management Group, about what was happening on the American golf scene, and my future agent was telling him about his potential new client. Picturing a player who is large, strong, and blond, Lawrence referred to me as the Golden Bear.

By 1963, sportswriters and other media types often identified me as the Golden Bear, or just the Bear, and as I developed a business beyond just playing golf, the name suited me well in other capacities. While my company has changed names from Golden Bear International to the Nicklaus Companies, my office is still located not far from my house in North Palm Beach, Florida, in Golden Bear Plaza. Our golf course design firm, Nicklaus Design, has been fortunate to be involved with more than three hundred golf courses worldwide, and there are probably a few dozen of them that have Bear somewhere in the name. In fact, my home club in Florida is called The Bear's Club.

This was the golf bag I used in my final U.S. Open, at Pebble Beach in 2000.

memorable ACES

HERE'S THE GOLF BALL FROM MY FIRST ACE AS A PROFESSIONAL. It's the old Tourney ball made by MacGregor. Keeping this golf ball in no way reflects the quality of the shot I hit that day, May 27, 1963, on the third hole at Colonial Country Club during the Memphis Invitational in Memphis, Tennessee. (Colonial, by the way, is the course where Al Geiberger shot the first 59 on the PGA Tour.)

Let me tell you about my hole-in-one: It wasn't a very good shot. I hit a 6-iron, if you can call what I did hitting the ball. The pin was in the back left and I didn't finish my swing, and the ball was going right all the way. But it bounced off a knob on the front right portion of the green, and then it shot diagonally across the putting surface and went in the hole. It was a horrible shot, really.

I scored my very first ace when I was thirteen years old and playing in the junior club championship at Scioto against a very nice golfer, Bill Cowman. We got through to the seventeenth hole our first time around in the thirty-six-hole final, and he hit it in there about a foot or two from the hole. Then I stepped up and knocked my shot in the hole with an 8-iron. The second time around on seventeen, he knocked it in close again and made a two and won the hole, and that squared the match. As he was walking off the green his father said to him, "See I told you if you kept making two, you'd win the hole." We all had a pretty good laugh.

I'm happy to say I had the last laugh, if you will. I won the match 1-up on the thirty-eighth hole, so that hole-in-one proved as valuable as it was memorable.

My first ace on a national stage came during a practice round at the USGA Juniors in 1956.

NAN'S BIRTH

I PLAYED IN A FUNDRAISER AT SCIOTO COUNTRY CLUB FOR THE AMERICAN CANCER SOCIETY WITH BOB HOPE, James Garner, and Walker Inman, the head pro at Scioto, in what was a forerunner of the Memorial Tournament. The date was May 4, 1965, and you'll understand momentarily why I remember the date. It was a nice day in Columbus, and I enjoyed our foursome very much, and, of course, we were playing for a good cause.

Barbara was pregnant with Nan at the time, and it was very late in her pregnancy, so she rode along on the golf course in a cart. Afterwards, we all went over to our house on Abington Road for dinner. This included Bob and Jim and some of the folks from the American Cancer Society.

Here's Nan when she was ten years old, dressed just like a true fan of Scottish golf.

A short time after we got home, I told Barb that we were going to go down in the basement and play some pool. She asked if I could first go out and start up the fire in the grill. "Oh, I'll be up in a few minutes to fix the fire," I said. This was in the days when you took the charcoal bricks and sprinkled lighter fluid on them and got a fire going; there were no gas grills then. About a half hour later, she called down and asked if I could cook the steaks. "Cook the steaks? But, I haven't fixed the fire." Well, she had gone ahead and fixed the fire. About another half hour went by, and she called down again and said that dinner was on the table. "It is? But I haven't cooked the steaks," I said. She said, "That's OK, I cooked the steaks. No big deal."

We sat down at the table, and now it was probably around eight-thirty in the evening. At about nine, we were sitting around chatting, and Barbara got up, excused herself, and went into the bedroom. Quite a bit of time went by, more than a half hour, and I started to wonder, what in the world is Barbara doing? I went to the back of the house and she said, "Well, I've got my bag packed and I've called the doctor. Do you want to take me to the hospital or should I call a taxi?" I was flabbergasted. I said, "Why didn't you tell me what was going on?" So I went back in the dining room to tell everyone I was taking Barb to the hospital, and believe me, you never saw a room clear out so fast. Zip . . . everybody was gone.

I went back in the dining room to tell everyone I was taking Barb to the hospital, and believe me, you never saw a room clear out so fast.

On the way to Ohio State University Hospital, we decided that if it were a boy, we would name the baby Robert James—after Bob Hope and Jim Garner. Nan was born at 12:15 a.m. on May 5. I, of course, fainted when they brought her in. I did that with all my children. Barbara's doctor, William Copeland, even followed me in his car later that night to make sure I got home OK.

The end of the story is that Nan, who later married Bill O'Leary, a former linebacker on the University of Georgia football team, named the fourth of their five children Robert James. She and Bill had heard the story so many times, they decided to use the name.

the BIG THREE

NOT LONG AFTER MEETING HIM, Gary Player became my closest friend during our time to-gether on Tour. Arnold Palmer and I have grown very close through the years, but the truth is that even during the period when we were going at each other head-to-head, we were always good friends.

Because of our collective success on the golf course—from 1958-66, we combined to win eight of nine Masters, as well as other major tournaments—we were known as the Big Three. Our notable achievements, plus our common business relationship with Mark McCormack of

The Big Three, shown here in 1963.

International Management Group, created opportunities for us to spend time together and to take advantage of our marketability. One of those financial ventures was a series of exhibitions and made-for-TV matches. We enjoyed our time together very much, not only joining forces for special events, but also traveling and doing other things.

Gary and I were no doubt closer because of our common interests and our penchant for needling each other mercilessly, plus we were closer in age than we were to Arnold. Gary is only four years older than I am, while Arnold is ten years my senior. Our families have become quite close, too; Gary has six kids to my five, plus a healthy array of grandchildren.

I think what Gary has accomplished in golf—nine majors and well over 150 worldwide titles—considering his small stature and the amount of travel he's had, is just phenomenal. He's probably put more air miles on his body than any person in history. He's been awfully good for a long time. And he's handled himself so well in some difficult situations. Gary Player really is an ambassador—a great ambassador for his country and for the game of golf.

I was trying to beat the man who represented the best player in the game. It could have been anybody. It just happened to be Arnold Palmer, probably the most popular champion the game has ever seen.

Arnold, of course, has been no less an ambassador for golf, as well as for sportsmanship and American ideals, and there's no doubt his overwhelming popularity helped grow the game tremendously as television was becoming the dominant medium. When I came on the scene, Arnold was the guy at the top of the hill. All I was trying to do was see if I could climb that hill myself, and there were a lot of fans who didn't like to see their hero challenged.

I don't think there is any question that early on, I wore a black hat to Arnold's white, but I think anyone who came along would have worn a black hat in comparison. I think that turned around some for me when I won the 1965 Masters. People appreciated what I did, the kind of golf I was playing. But it wasn't necessarily Arnold, per se, I was intent on beating. I was trying

to beat the man who represented the best player in the game. It could have been anybody. It just happened to be Arnold Palmer, probably the most popular champion the game has ever seen.

Honestly, though I might have had to battle Arnie's Army, I never had to battle Arnold Palmer. He couldn't have treated me any better when I joined the Tour. His graciousness was nothing short of amazing, and I've held the deepest respect and admiration for him since the beginning. I'm not sure that if the tables were turned I could have been quite as gracious as he was, though I think my dad would have expected nothing less and I'd have come around.

These days, though the three of us are running in a million different directions with our larger families and business interests, we remain as close as ever. I know that if I ever needed Gary or Arnold for anything, they would be there for me in a heartbeat, and they know I would be there for them.

Though we battled each other throughout our careers, Arnold, Gary, and I have always remained close friends.

AUGUSTA NATIONAL GOLF CLUB

ONE OF THE NEATEST THINGS ABOUT THE MASTERS TOURNAMENT—and there are nine

million things that make the Masters great—is its adherence to certain traditions, and I'm a huge

believer in tradition. One tradition that still gives me goose bumps is taking the short drive down

Magnolia Lane to the clubhouse of Augusta National Golf Club. It happened to me again earlier

this year, even though I attended the Masters in a non-competing capacity.

Another great tradition is of a tangible nature: the awarding of gifts at the end of the week.

Granted, the most coveted gifts that you strive for are the green jacket and the winner's trophy.

But Augusta National, of which I am proud to say I am now a member, has been generous in

passing out other valuable keepsakes, such as gold medals to the low amateurs and silver medals

to the tournament runner-up. In 1954, the club began the practice of awarding crystal pieces for

various achievements, such as low round of the day, eagles, or holes-in-one.

I never paid attention to the number of items Augusta has given to me, not that they didn't

mean anything. On the contrary, each meant a great deal. The Masters was the first tournament

that I really recall anything about—I was probably about thirteen or fourteen years old. And when

I was first invited to the Masters in 1959 as a member of the U.S. Walker Cup team, I couldn't wait

Above is a bag tag from the 1972 Masters.

HOLE	Prev	1	2	3	4	5	6	7	8	9	10	11	12	13	14	15	16	17	18
PAR	Score	4	5	4	3	4	3	4	5	4	4	4	3	5	4	5	4	3	4
PALMER	6	6	6	6	5	5	4	5	6	6	6								
AARON	3	3	2	2	2	2	2	2	2	2	0								
SANDERS	3	3	4	3	1	1	1	2	2	2									
CASPER											1	2	2						
LEMA	4	4	3	1	2	2	2	1	0	0	0	1	0						
PLAYER	8	8	9		7	7	7	7	8	8	7	7	6						
RUDOLPH	1	1		0	1	0	0	0	1	2	3	4	4	5	5	5	5	5	
SIKES, D.			4	4	4	4	4	5	5	6	6	6	6	7					
NICKLAUS	6	6	7	7	8	9	10	11	11	11	11	11	12	13					
LITTLER			3	1	1	1	1	2	2	3	4	4	4	4	3	3	3		

NOTES

J MARTIN

RIVERS

to get down there. The influence of Jones always made it so special, and the beauty and challenge of the course always had a way of inspiring me. But it just never occurred to me to add up all the nifty keepsakes. Counting to six was always fun, I can tell you that, and I wish I could have counted even higher, as far as first-place finishes go. I was surprised to find out not long ago that I had won eighty-eight individual keepsakes in my forty-five Masters appearances—a pretty good average.

To sit here and think about what I did to earn each of these might take awhile. I received a silver-gold cup, a gold medal, and a silver cigarette box engraved with my name on it when I

I was surprised to find out not long ago that I had won eighty-eight individual keepsakes in my forty-five Masters appearances—a pretty good average.

---

finished in a tie for thirteenth place in the 1960 Masters, with Ted Kroll and another amateur, William J. Patton, who received similar presents. My first crystal awards, two highball glasses, came in 1962, when I eagled the par-five thirteenth hole in the second round.

Obviously, I can always pick out certain other occasions, like the 64 I shot in round three of the 1965 Masters, one of the finest rounds of golf I ever played. Not only did I receive a crystal vase for that round, the low round of the day, but I got another for a final-round 69 that propelled me to my second green jacket with a tournament record 271 aggregate score, nine strokes better than my good friends and top rivals, Arnold Palmer and Gary Player.

Thirty years later, while Ben Crenshaw won his second Masters title in 1995, I was busy writing an interesting footnote by eagling the par-four fifth hole twice in three days. Number Five, named Magnolia, is a dogleg left, with deep bunkers guarding the left side of the fairway and a heavily sloping green with a false front. These days it measures 455 yards. It's never been an easy birdie hole—I carded only ten birdies there in my Masters career—and it ranks among the

---

Holing a putt on the way to a 271 in the 1965 Masters, one of the most commanding performances of my career.

toughest half-dozen holes on the course over the history of the tournament. But in 1995, I guess I had its number. In the first round I knocked my second shot into the hole with a 7-iron. I returned on Saturday and made another eagle, this time with a 5-iron. For that feat I earned a trip to the interview room and two pairs of crystal glasses.

Now for the true accounting of things: I actually have received eighty-nine Masters-related keepsakes. Pictured here is the one piece that was overlooked, and one not many people know exists, yet it has significant meaning: It's a gold locket in the shape of the logo of Augusta National Golf Club that was given to me by Ben Hogan after I won the 1963 Masters. Hogan started the tradition of the Masters Club and the annual Champions Dinner held on Tuesday night of tournament week, and he gave me my locket at the dinner in '64. Hogan thought that whenever someone won the Masters, they should have a locket to signify they belong to that club. Byron

Hogan started the tradition of the Masters Club and the annual Champions Dinner held on Tuesday night of tournament week, and he gave me my locket at the dinner in '64.

Nelson eventually took over those duties once Ben stopped coming to Augusta, and Ben Crenshaw took over this past year to fulfill Byron's wishes. Byron missed the Masters for the first time since 1935, and we missed him greatly, but Ben did a wonderful job as the new host.

It's traditions like these that make the Masters what it is and only add to what I consider the greatest game of all.

This locket (above) represents membership in an exclusive club. Previous: My third Masters victory in 1966 gave me an opportunity to practice my dance steps.

the MAJOR CHAMPIONSHIPS

THROUGHOUT MY CAREER, whatever golf tournament I entered was the most important thing in my mind that week. I always played to win and I always played with maximum effort, not only because of my competitive nature, but also because the people who hosted the tournament and the folks who came to watch me play deserved to see me trying my darndest to win.

There was never a doubt in my mind, however, that certain tournaments are bigger than others and mean more. Of course, those are the four major championships: the Masters Tournament, the United States Open Championship, the British Open, and the PGA Championship. I always felt like the major championships really defined a player, and those were the tournaments in which I most wanted to excel. Bob Jones, though a career amateur, essentially prepared his game every summer for winning the most important championships of his day: the U.S. Open, the U.S. Amateur, the British Open, and the British Amateur. In 1960, after he won the Masters and the U.S. Open, Arnold Palmer went to St. Andrews to try and win the British Open after years in which most top American professionals had stopped entering, and the modern version of the Grand Slam was established.

The Wanamaker trophies, from my PGA Championship victories in 1963, 1971, 1973, 1975, and 1980.

Arnold understood the importance of major titles to a player's record. No one ever had to convince me that he and Jones got it right. The majors are the biggest tournaments that you strive to win. In most people's minds, the majors are sort of beyond their comprehension, because they mean so much. That's why major championships are the toughest to win. In another sense however, I can honestly say they're also the easiest to win, and by that I mean that if a guy can get his act together, he can get a leg up psychologically.

I think the ideal of what goes into making a tournament a major championship is that they are supposed to be difficult. The majors are supposed to take more, physically and mentally,

I think the ideal of what goes into making a tournament a major championship is that they are supposed to be difficult. The majors are supposed to take more, physically and mentally, to win than any other tournament.

to win than any other tournament. They're supposed to be a total examination, on a fair but challenging golf course. Winning a major is supposed to be about many things; it's not only the driving, but also the iron play, the short game, the putting, the test of your composure, your preparation, your approach, your attitude and toughness. It's about knowing when to back off, knowing when to get aggressive, and knowing that you're facing all these challenges while playing against the world's best players, the very best competition. Every player has an equal chance to win. They are special events, and knowing you're only going to play four of those a year adds to the pressure, and I always truly enjoyed that pressure and competition. That's the significance of the major championships.

My attitude about major championships was pretty straightforward. I never made it a secret that I wanted to win as many as I could, and early on I set my sights on trying to break Jones' record of thirteen major titles. Every spring I also had in the back of my mind the ultimate prize:

The Wanamaker Trophy is not exactly a trinket. Here I am hefting it for the fifth time, in 1980, at Oak Hill Country Club in Rochester, New York.

the Grand Slam. Jones had won his version of it in 1930, and then retired. Seven times I began

the year winning the first major championship (in 1971 the PGA was played in February, which

I won at PGA National, close to my home), and twice I came close. In 1972 I won the Masters and

the U.S. Open, then watched Lee Trevino chip in to beat me by a stroke at the British Open at

Muirfield. In '75, I probably came the closest when I ran off this streak: Masters, first; U.S. Open,

seventh; British Open, third; PGA Championship, first. I missed playoffs in the U.S. Open and

British Open by a combined three strokes.

I've said many times that I always thought the start of the golfing year came at the Masters

(with the exception of that '71 PGA), and everything that I did prior to that was to prepare myself for

One of the better-known shots of my career: the 1-iron that glanced off the flagstick on the 17th at Pebble Beach, to win the 1972 U.S. Open. Previous: The last tee at Augusta National Golf Club.

Augusta National Golf Club. I always started in January picking tournaments I wanted to play that would give me the necessary competition and maybe similar conditions to what I might encounter at Augusta. I played courses that might afford the opportunity to play shots that I would probably play at Augusta, places where you needed to fly the ball in the air, which was always important at Augusta. I tended to avoid tournaments where there might be a ton of wind and you'd have to play a lot of knockdown shots and make adjustments that wouldn't be useful in my preparations. Occasionally, I'd play in them if there was something specifically I thought I still needed to sharpen, but mostly I tended to stick with the places I wanted to play. I always first organized my schedule around golf courses with the majors in mind.

When I arrived at Augusta I wanted to still be building my game, so that I knew I was focused on the things I wanted to do. I wanted that for all the majors, building up to them right into the week, so I always felt like I was trying to climb a mountain and be as sharp as I could be, both physically and mentally. Then it was just a matter of knowing how to play the course. The philosophy of Augusta is that it is a position golf course, a second-shot course. You want to drive the ball on the proper side of the fairways to give yourself the best angles to get at the hole. It was important to learn what you had to do and what to avoid. You always knew you would encounter fast greens and perfect conditions and a beautiful setting; all of that plays into how you prepare.

After building toward competing in the Masters and then playing in the tournament, I would try to bring myself back down, take a bit of a breather, collect my thoughts and reenergize, and then move on to preparing for the next major championship, which was the U.S. Open. I started thinking: What kind of golf course are we playing in the U.S. Open? And what was the challenge I would encounter? Then I would start honing my game and playing shots and the golf courses that would prepare me. It was common for me to go into the U.S. Open venue a week or so before, so I could play practice rounds and get a feel for the golf course, its conditions and challenges. Then I'd do the same thing for the British Open, although you couldn't get the conditions and the types of golf courses here in the States that you have in Scotland and England; nevertheless, the thought process was the same. I'd go over the week before and acclimate myself to the weather, the different

kinds of courses we would play, and the shots I would need. Then I'd put myself through the paces yet again for the PGA Championship. That, essentially, was my year; that's what I always prepared for. After the PGA, I didn't play a lot of golf until January, when I would start from scratch and repeat the process of building my golf game.

I don't know how many other guys did that, but that was my routine, and that's how I kept myself playing and how I kept myself interested; how I kept kicking myself in the rear end just to get going. I never worried about how other players prepared. I knew what worked for me, and what worked for me might not work for someone else. That reflects the nature of golf itself: Every individual has a different way of doing things.

But we all are trying to accomplish the same thing. We want to win. And we know what it means to win the biggest events in the game. If you look back over time, the major championships are the events in which you can compare golfers of yesterday with golfers of today. Because of the advances in equipment, you can't possibly compare the overall game I played, or even the one Ben Hogan or Gene Sarazen or Bob Jones played, with the game that is being played today.

We will always have the majors, however. You can compare major champions as far back as the game has been played. They are the only measuring stick, really, of assessing golfers of any era, and the majors are what connect golfers of every era.

Willie Peterson and I celebrate the forty-foot putt that all but wrapped up the 1975 Masters.

the RYDER CUP

MY INDIVIDUAL RECORD IN THE RYDER CUP, a decent 17–8–3 overall, but an ordinary 4–4–2 in singles play, in no way reflects how I feel about the event.

I have considered it a tremendous honor to play for my country in the biennial matches that at first pitted players from the United States against professional golfers from Great Britain and later against a team that included continental Europe. In addition to five appearances as a player for America, I captained two teams. Regardless of my role, I wanted to win every time. It is a competition, after all. My firm belief, however, has always been that the matches are meant to be played in the spirit of goodwill and sportsmanship, and that ideal superseded everything, including a win-only mentality.

I've had some terrific memories of the Ryder Cup. The most vivid of those would have to be the 1969 matches at Royal Birkdale Golf Club in Southport, England, which ended in a 16-16 tie, the first tie in the history of the event. It all came down to my match with England's Tony Jacklin, who was the reigning British Open champion at the time. Tony whipped me pretty good in morning singles, 4 and 3, and we battled back and forth in the afternoon. At the last, with our match all square, I faced a four-foot par putt, while he was two feet away. After I made mine, I picked up his marker and conceded the putt. I told him, "I don't believe you would have missed that, but I'd never give you the opportunity under the circumstances."

I learned later that Sam Snead, our captain, was less than thrilled with my decision, but we retained the cup with the tie, since the U.S. had won the match in 1967—and twelve of the previous thirteen. Leo Fraser, president of the PGA of America, obviously felt as I did, and left the Ryder Cup for the British team to hold for a year. In my mind, conceding the putt to Tony, who was a hero at home, was the right thing to do, the only thing I could do, given my sentiments

toward the matches as goodwill exhibitions. (Recently, I had the pleasure of collaborating on a golf course with Tony in Sarasota, Florida, called The Concession.)

The U.S. team went back to dominating the Ryder Cup after '69, to the point where I was genuinely worried about the future of the event and its relevance in the game. In 1977, at the matches at Royal Lytham and St. Annes, England, I had a chance to sit down one night with Lord John

My concession to Tony Jacklin in the 1969 Ryder Cup.

Derby, the president of the British PGA, and I said, "John, you know that everyone from the American team thinks it's a great honor to play in the matches, but frankly, when the matches start, there isn't much competition. We win every year, and I don't think that's right." I suggested that the pool of players from the opposing side be expanded from Great Britain and Ireland (Irish players were

first eligible to make the team in 1973) to include continental Europe, and the idea was adopted in time for the 1979 matches.

Since then, the Ryder Cup has been one of the most fervently contested golf events in the world, and the addition of all of Europe has resulted in a shift in the results, starting in 1987, when I captained the U.S. team and saw that fine squad fall for the first time on American soil to a strong European contingent. The loss occurred, of all places, at Muirfield Village Golf Club, the course I designed just outside my hometown of Columbus. But that was fine. It was great for golf and a great thing for the Ryder Cup, a real turning point.

It's been distressing for me, however, to see the Ryder Cup become, in the last decade or so, too much of an out-and-out rivalry, with a notable lack of friendliness and goodwill. That's not what the Ryder Cup should become, and I hope that doesn't happen to the Presidents Cup, which pits the U.S. versus golfers from all over the world, except Europe. Golf is still a game. It's not a war.

The Ryder Cup and the Presidents Cup matches are opportunities for the best players in the world to compete, but more important, they are opportunities to showcase and expand the game to fans all over the world, and to display the goodwill and sportsmanship that is at the foundation of golf, which is what makes our game so special.

Hopefully, the Ryder Cup will retain the sportsmanship upon which it was established.

the 1973 PGA CHAMPIONSHIP

WHEN I WON THE 1970 BRITISH OPEN AT ST. ANDREWS TO END A MAJOR CHAMPIONSHIP DROUGHT OF THREE YEARS, Bob Green, a longtime golf writer for the Associated Press, was there to greet me in the interview room with surprising news. "Jack, congratulations, that's ten," Bob said. "Only three more to tie Bob Jones." Though I had long ago said that bettering Jones' record of thirteen major championships was a goal of mine once I fully committed to becoming a golfer, I had, honestly, never bothered to count them up. It had never occurred to me. Poor Tiger Woods. Today, with so much media attention focused on him, they've been counting since he won his first major.

Fortunately, the knowledge of where I stood in relation to Jones didn't affect me adversely. I won the 1971 PGA and the 1972 Masters and U.S. Open for half a Slam. Then, as the 1973 season commenced, I became a little more fixated on breaking the record, not to mention adding to my streak of years winning a major. Jones' record always had been in the back of my mind, but I just had never allowed myself to think about it. Now I was thinking about it.

My favorite photograph: carrying Gary off the green after the second round of the 1973 PGA Championship.

My putting in the middle rounds let me down in the Masters, as Tommy Aaron captured the green jacket, and torrid golf by Johnny Miller at the U.S. Open at Oakmont (Johnny shot a record 63 in the final round) and by Tom Weiskopf at the British Open at Royal Troon gave each man a well-deserved breakthrough victory. That left me with the PGA Championship as my last shot that year, and as smiling fate would have it, the PGA was scheduled to be played at Canterbury Golf Club in the Cleveland suburb of Beachwood, where family members and countless friends could watch me try to win another major in my home state.

Jones' record always had been in the back of my mind, but I just had never allowed myself to think about it. Now I was thinking about it.

I eventually won the PGA by four strokes over Bruce Crampton. The accolades that followed were flattering, but also a bit unsettling, because people seemed to dismiss what Jones had accomplished before me. My intention was always to be the best I could be and to try and break his record—not eclipse his memory or the memory of other great golfers before me.

One memory that cannot be eclipsed in my mind was what occurred after my second-round 68 at Canterbury. Because we were so close to home and had so many friends and relatives on hand, Barbara and I decided to take a chance and bring our four oldest children to the tournament. As perpetually busy as I was as a child, our kids were equally energetic, but we figured the vastly superior number of adults watching them would sufficiently stunt any potential for playful mischief. This was one time we miscalculated—and I'd have to say I'm glad we did.

As I putted out on the eighteenth hole Friday afternoon, Jackie, our oldest, instructed Gary, who was four years old, to run out on the green. "Look, there's your dad, go on out and give him a big hug," Jackie said. Gary happily obliged and I scooped him up with one arm and carried him off. A photographer captured the moment and won an award for his timely snapshot.

I got something much more valuable—and it had nothing to do with Bob Jones and breaking records. That photo remains perhaps my favorite from my golf career.

MUIRFIELD VILLAGE GOLF CLUB

TEE 1				TIME 10:14								1976								PREVIOUS TOTAL	

CONTESTANT JACK NICKLAUS — the Memorial Tournament — OFFICIAL SCORE CARD — MUIRFIELD VILLAGE GOLF CLUB, DUBLIN, OHIO

DATE May 27, 1976 — THIS ROUND / NEW TOTAL

HOLES	1	2	3	4	5	6	7	8	9	OUT	HOLES	10	11	12	13	14	15	16	17	18	IN	TOTAL
YARDS	433	452	392	214	540	430	549	174	393	3577	YARDS	441	538	158	442	355	490	204	430	437	3495	7072
PAR	4	4	4	3	5	4	5	3	4	36	PAR	4	5	3	4	4	5	3	4	4	36	72
SCORE	4	5	4	3	3	3	6	2	5		SCORE	3	6	2	4	3	4	3	5	6		
										35											36	71

MARKER'S SIGNATURE   CONTESTANT'S SIGNATURE

WE ALL HAVE OUR GRAND DREAMS AND VISIONS, and one of mine that began to germinate not long after I became a professional golfer was to someday build my own golf club in Columbus. Not only did I want to contribute something to my hometown by bringing a top-flight golf tournament to central Ohio, I also had a keen desire to give something back to the game.

Muirfield Village Golf Club is the dream that became a reality. We opened Muirfield Village—its name is derived from Muirfield, the course of the Honourable Company of Edinburgh Golfers where I won my first British Open—in 1974, but it physically started taking shape almost a decade earlier, when I talked to longtime friends Pandel Savic and Ivor Young about what I wanted to do. I asked Ivor, during a private conversation at the 1966 Masters, to find the land on which I eventually designed the golf course.

The first Memorial Tournament was held in 1976, and the idea behind the event was to not only host a PGA Tour event, but also to use the occasion of an annual golf gathering to honor figures who had made a significant contribution to the game. Our inaugural honoree was Bob Jones.

Through the years I think the Memorial has become a pretty good tournament, and I think the practice of honoring golfers and other important people in the history of the game has been a wonderful bonus to it all. Granted, we've had some battles with weather coming out of spring, but that's about the only complaint I can think of. We've tried to run a first-rate event, and we took

My scorecard from the first Memorial Tournament.

our cues from another well-run tournament, the Masters. Cliff Roberts, who cofounded Augusta National Golf Club with Bob Jones, was one of the original members of our Captains Club, the group that sets tournament policy. He opened up everything to us that we would want. Our people went down and talked to his people, and we saw how a well-organized tournament is run. After only a short time, Roberts made a statement to me that I thought was really quite nice. He said, "Jack, you have an opportunity to do in ten years what has taken us forty at Augusta."

There have been a lot of lessons learned at this tournament as a result of experience, and I certainly don't have to do as much as I did in the early years. We've always been fortunate to have great people involved and a marvelous volunteer contingent.

Where I have kept busiest is with the evolution of the golf course. I had been involved in the design of only nine courses when I undertook the building of Muirfield Village. Pete Dye helped

A dream come true: the opening of the first Memorial Tournament in 1976.

me with selecting the site, and he and Desmond Muirhead contributed to the routing, but the rest was up to me. Through the years I have made a lot of changes to the course, some for the sake of the members, some to improve the spectator experience, and some simply to make the golf course a better and stronger test. Muirfield Village can be a difficult golf course, and with the remarkable changes in equipment, I've done my share of tinkering to keep it from becoming obsolete. I've spent a ton of time on that golf course, but it's a labor of love, and I haven't changed the course radically. Like any designer, I want the course to show well, and be able to hold up against the game's best players, so I have tried to find ways to preserve shot values. Nevertheless, other than adding some necessary distance and totally reworking the seventeenth hole, Muirfield Village is the same course that opened in 1974. Like Augusta, Muirfield is primarily a second-shot golf course, with wide playing corridors and well-protected greens. Muirfield is still a course where placing the ball in the proper areas is more important than power. I think that makes for more exciting golf, and we've had our fair share of fantastic finishes through the years, not to mention a good roll call of champions.

I've poured most of my life for the last forty-plus years into what's happened with the golf club, the tournament, and the golf course, and it's been a fairly emotional thing for me. There was a time when it almost didn't happen, when I put myself at serious financial risk trying to make it happen. I managed to get through it, however, thanks to good people around me, and my own stubbornness.

I may have retired from competitive golf, but I have said that I retain the right to come back and play in the Memorial Tournament, and I will probably do that at some point. I can't think of anything else that I've been more completely involved in, other than my family and playing golf, than Muirfield Village. I think it would be only fitting that the last official event I ever compete in is the Memorial. I know Sam Snead holds the record for the oldest player to make the cut in a Tour event. He was sixty-eight years old. So there you go, there's a goal. There's something to work toward.

There's no feeling like making a dream come true.

a MEMORABLE MEMORIAL

BEN HOGAN SUPPOSEDLY SAID AFTER MY RUNNER-UP FINISH AT THE 1960 U.S. OPEN THAT

IF I'D HAD A BRAIN IN MY HEAD, I'd have won by ten shots. I expressed similar sentiments about

myself on a couple of occasions, namely after the 1986 Masters, when I said I should have retired

Barbara and I with the 1977 Memorial Tournament trophy, one of the most meaningful victories of my career.

then and there, "if I had a brain in my head." But the very first time I had that thought was nine years earlier, on May 23, 1977, when I won the second edition of the Memorial Tournament.

I thought then, and I still believe today, that winning my own tournament was probably the most difficult victory I ever had in the game of golf. All the things that I was doing with the golf tournament—it was practically everything but parking cars and picking up the trash. Actually, I did a lot of that, too. My son Jackie was my caddie, and by the time we finished each round, his pockets were filled with cigarette butts and paper and things we had picked

---

I thought then, and I still believe today, that winning my own tournament was probably the most difficult victory I ever had in the game of golf.

---

up around the golf course. When I finished my final round on Monday—yes, Monday, after a weather delay—with a one-under-par 71, and 281 total, good for a two-stroke victory over Hubert Green, I don't think I was ever more exhausted after any other tournament I'd competed in, majors included.

I even mentioned to Barbara during the awards ceremony that I was thinking of announcing my retirement from competitive golf. After all, I had told Arnold Palmer years before that I'd be done with tournament golf by the time I was thirty-five, and here I was already two years past that predicted date. Fortunately, Barbara wisely counseled me to ignore the emotions I was battling at that moment and to bite my tongue.

To have won this golf tournament, with the worries and responsibilities I had at the time—the things that I was doing to make sure that every facet of the tournament was running not just well, but as close to perfect as we could get it, including the condition and setup of the golf course I designed—the pressure was enormous, but the payoff was a swell of pride that's seldom been equaled. I'm not exaggerating when I say it was my biggest thrill in golf. And I liked that feeling so much that I won the tournament again in 1984.

ANGELO ARGEA

I FIRST MET ANGELO IN 1963, in Palm Springs, California. The truth is I was stuck with him—or him with me. I had just missed my first cut as a professional in San Francisco after hurting my hip, and I was playing a few practice holes out of a cart at Indian Wells Country Club, in preparation for the Palm Springs Golf Classic, when the caddie master marched out to inform me, "Jack, I've got the caddie who's been assigned to you for the tournament." Of course, I knew they didn't assign caddies for tournaments back then, but I played along and said, "OK, I'll give him a try." That caddie was Angelo. It was sort of a con job, but I let them con me, because as it turned out, I won the golf tournament.

I liked Angelo right away, and I liked the results we achieved together. We won the tournament that week in Palm Springs in a playoff, and three months later I asked him to caddie for me in Las Vegas at the Tournament of Champions. Angelo lived in Las Vegas and was driving a taxi at the time. I opened with a 64 and we won again. We finished twentieth the following year at Palm Springs, but the next week there we were again in first place at the Phoenix Open. Then we rattled off two more wins: I successfully defended at the Tournament of Champions in Las Vegas, and later that year I captured the Portland Open with Angelo on the bag. Over the next few years he gradually became my full-time caddie.

He and I teamed to win quite a few tournaments together, probably close to fifty, and he worked for me regularly until the late 1970s. Angelo's practice was to go out early in the morning and get the pin locations for me. He knew enough of the golf course and my golf game that he was always a great help. Any information I needed he generally had. But I think it is at least as important that the player and the caddie have compatible personalities; Angelo and I always had a very good rapport. People always thought Angelo wore two watches while he worked—sometimes, when he

was running behind or had overslept, I wished he had three—but, no, it was his practice to keep my watch safe by wearing it. Sometimes when things weren't going quite the way I'd have liked them to, Ang could find some way to lift my spirits. Sometimes he merely would say to me, "Isn't it about time for a song?" That would get me singing or humming under my breath, and I'd start to feel better and get back to the task at hand.

His personality was such that I think he really enjoyed being in the spotlight a bit, carrying my bag. I remember when we were together when I won the 1980 U.S. Open at Baltusrol, and the people there were going absolutely bonkers, Angelo told me that was about as much fun as he ever had. He and I last worked together about ten years ago; he asked to caddie for me one more time, so we teamed up at the Senior PGA Championship at PGA National in Palm Beach Gardens, Florida. Angelo eventually started doing yardage books for some of the golf courses we designed, and he was able to use his personality to sell his services to a lot of clients.

He had a lot of personality and he had a real flair about him, but Angelo also was an excellent caddie.

I don't think Angelo ever had an enemy. He had friends everywhere, and he was like a part of our family until he died late in 2005. I can't tell you how many places I would go over the years and people would ask, "How's Angelo?" He was probably as recognizable as any player on the golf course, with that shock of silver hair and prominent mustache. He was one of the game's all-time great characters. He had a lot of personality and he had a real flair about him, but Angelo also was an excellent caddie. I enjoyed his company very much, and I think he enjoyed mine.

I know he enjoyed the limelight.

Angelo and I at the 1978 PGA Championship at Oakmont Country Club in Oakmont, Pennsylvania.

AUTOGRAPHS

THOUGH THE CONCEPT OF AUTO-GRAPHS HAS CHANGED OVER THE YEARS, my overall philosophy toward signing them has remained largely the same since it first became apparent quite a long time ago that folks were interested in having me sign various items and memorabilia.

These days I still enjoy it im-mensely, and when I make public appearances, I budget a certain amount of time to try to ac-commodate people, but I'm inclined to gauge how much time I'm willing to devote based on how folks are behaving. If everyone is respectful and patient, not just with me but also to one another, then I'm happy to hang around.

In addition, a few moments in the office or on my airplane, Air Bear, might be spent fulfilling various requests, which I'm happy to do. It seems like every time I get on my plane, my secretary is handing me a briefcase full of photos and magazines, cards, and more often than not these days, bank notes, which I'll talk about later.

Like I said, however, the concept of autographs has changed. I think it's unfortunate that a handful of people who ask me to sign an autograph might have ulterior motives. It used to be that folks sought an autograph for a keepsake, or because they were honored to meet you, or because it

I've always tried to accommodate autograph seekers throughout my career.

was their hobby. Now you have the occasional "collector" whose only real motivation is putting that flag or photo that I've signed on eBay as fast as he can post it, so that he can earn a few dollars. That doesn't make me very happy. I've also had to spend quite a bit of my own money, as have Tiger and Arnold, among other athletes, to take steps to protect my name and guard against misuse of my signature.

But I'm never going to let a few troublemakers ruin what I think is a neat thing to do for people, and quite frankly, something I still consider an honor. I learned a long time ago that it's part of the deal; it's a responsibility that goes with my position as an athlete and a role

model. I can recall playing in an exhibition in Cincinnati not long after I turned professional. Bob Hope was there, and I was amazed at how he handled the large group of people tugging at him. He was very patient and made a little bit of time for everyone. It made quite an impression on me.

I could say that I have tried to put myself in other people's shoes, but the fact is I once *was* in their shoes. I had just started playing golf in 1950 when the PGA Championship came to Scioto Country Club. I managed to find my way into the locker room, which was a pretty big deal for a ten-year-old kid. I found Lloyd Mangrum sitting at a table with a drink in one hand and cards in the other, and a cigarette was dangling from his mouth. He looked up at me and said in this gravelly voice, "Whadda ya want kid?" But he signed my autograph book. So did Sam Snead and Cary Middlecoff and a few others. I did pretty well.

Still have them, too. No, I never wondered what I could get for them on eBay. They mean too much to the ten-year-old kid in me that got them.

A page from my old autograph book, started in 1950.

Through the years I have enjoyed corresponding with lots of terrific people, the famous and not so famous, strangers as well as good friends.

THE WHITE HOUSE
WASHINGTON
6-23-94

Dear Jack —

I'm sorry you couldn't make the State Dinner. Hope you will be able to come while I'm here.

I enjoyed watching you and pulling for you in the US Open.

Meanwhile I'll keep working on my golf game and the economy! Both are in better shape than when we were together, though the golf is still more unpredictable than the international currency markets!

Sincerely
Bill Clinton

FRANK SINATRA
March 16, 1995

Dear Jack,

Many thanks for your generosity in donating an item for auction at our recent golf tournament. Everyone associated with the February 24 and February 25 Frank Sinatra Celebrity Golf Tournament, particularly those affiliated with the organizations our event benefits, are most appreciative.

The Barbara Sinatra Children's Center at Eisenhower Medical Center, and Palm Springs' Desert Hospital are facilities that treat those in need day-in and day-out and are integral parts of our community. Barbara and I are grateful to you for your support.

Best regards,
Frank Sinatra

a few LETTERS

GERALD R. FORD May 25th

Dear Jack:

Congratulations on your selection by the Captain's Club Memorial Honoree. Most regrettably I could not be at the ceremony where your superb record was appropriately recognized. You should be very, very proud of your terrific achievements of many years.

I thank you and Barbara for your countless kindnesses to Betty and me. We treasure our friendship with both of you.

Jerry Ford

I DON'T OWN AN I-POD AND I DON'T HAVE AN E-MAIL ADDRESS—though Barbara does. I refuse to carry a cell phone. CD players and DVD players make perfect sense. Progress is good, but I don't feel the need to buy all the latest gadgets that come along and clutter up my life. Besides, I was never that way with my golf, either. There's nothing wrong with good, old-fashioned U.S. mail. Barb and I still send out Christmas cards every year. Through the years I have enjoyed corresponding with lots of terrific people, the famous and not so famous, strangers as well as good friends. Here are letters from some of the more well-known folks that might interest readers. I sure enjoyed them.

Pictured are letters from Gerald Ford (above), Bill Clinton, and Frank Sinatra.

my love of FISHING

I HAVE LOVED FISHING OF EVERY KIND SINCE MY GOLF COACH AT OHIO STATE, Bob Kepler, introduced me to fly-casting. I think Kep would be happy to know that all these decades later, fishing is still one of my favorite leisure activities, though I'm not always fishing with relaxation in mind. I still find an awful lot of competition in trying to catch a fish properly, and now that I've stopped competing at golf, I get more satisfaction out of fishing. I fish all over the world, and coincidentally, a lot of golf courses that I select for my design firm usually are close to a place where the fishing is good. I promise you that I'm quite a bit better at fishing than I am at hitting a golf ball. After all, a bonefish doesn't know how old I am.

Naturally, I have a fish tale to share.

A few days prior to the 1978 Australian Open in Sydney, I caught a black marlin after a battle of six hours and twenty-five minutes. My arms and back were so tired and sore that I shot 73 in the first round of the tournament at the Australian Golf Club, a course I had recently redesigned. (I rallied the next three days, however, to win my sixth Australian Open title.) The fish I reeled

A 1965 Field & Stream *fishing contest certificate, good for third place.*

in was a better prize, though. You don't get many opportunities, if ever, to reel in a fish like this one. It was the largest black marlin in length ever caught off the coast of Australia—and still is. It was the fourth-largest by weight, tipping the scale at 1,358 pounds. Unfortunately, it had been out of the water for twelve hours before we could weigh it, and because of dehydration, it lost about 10 percent of its mass.

The story actually gets better. I had it shipped home in a crate that was the shape of the fish, with the pectoral fins sticking out of it, and at every port it went into, someone wrote a note on it, because my name was on the shipment. "Jack, nice going. Great catch." Whatever people could think of to say was on it. I still have the box. I had it displayed in the back of my office for about a year.

Not too long after I caught it, I decided to hang the fish over the fireplace. Now, the ceiling was only nine feet, and the fish had to be about five feet deep, and the pectoral fin was sticking out at about neck height. Barbara was good-humored about it. She let me keep it up there for a while, but she put a red flag on the fin so no one would get strangled or run into it.

Though I consider fishing a form of competition, sometimes I do manage to cast a line for relaxation as well.

DIVERSIONS

AS FAR BACK AS I CAN REMEMBER, since I was maybe six years old, I have had tremendous enthusiasm for sports. If I wasn't playing them, then I was watching, talking about or even dreaming about them. A popular myth is that I lived, breathed, and ate golf in my youth. The fact is that until about seventeen, golf, though a passion of mine, was one of many athletic pursuits.

Growing up in Columbus, my interests in sports moved with the seasons. I loved the core sports—football, basketball, and baseball—but there was also swimming and tennis, bowling, snow-sledding, plus hunting and fishing. The reason was simply a competitive drive and the desire to excel. Of course, golf superseded everything eventually. It was the one sport where I became good enough to compete at the highest level, and that has always charged my batteries.

I played a lot of sports as a kid, including baseball, basketball, and football.

One of the best things about golf, and probably why I ended up gravitating to it, is because it was a sport that I could do by myself and be as good as I wanted to be relying solely on my effort. I didn't have to have somebody throw the ball back to me or guard me or guard somebody else; I didn't need somebody else to play the game with. I love team sports. But this was an individual sport. It was just me against me and the golf course, and I liked that, and the challenge of self-reliance it demanded.

But to play golf solely, at a young age, never entered my mind. I think that all people need time away from their jobs, time to be able to clear their minds. As much as I loved golf, I needed to do that, too.

I discovered that before I ever started playing professional golf. Did I want to win? Absolutely. Did I want to work hard? Yeah, I wanted to work hard. Did I want to be the best player that I could be? Sure. I always wanted to be those things, but I didn't want that to be at the expense of my family and the many other interests I had. Here again you have to give credit to my father, who loved sports, but who never looked at life through that narrow prism. Life is about experiences, which make you a well-rounded individual and, hopefully, a better person.

I started playing golf when I was ten. Sure, I had success when I was young. I won tournaments when I was ten, eleven, twelve, thirteen—won tournaments all the way through. But I continued to play other sports. I was playing baseball, football, and basketball almost all the way through high school. I ran track. I was recruited for basketball in college, and I almost went to college to play basketball. But I went to Ohio State because I wanted to go to Ohio State, not to play golf. Ohio State didn't give golf scholarships, so I could have played basketball, but I didn't want to play, not with Jerry Lucas and John Havlicek—future NBA stars—on that team; I wouldn't have played much. I wanted to go to Ohio State because my friends went to Ohio State. I never missed an Ohio State football game from the time I was six years old, and I loved the basketball games, too. I wanted to be a student and be in a fraternity, and I wanted to taste college life.

I didn't care about being a great golfer when I was seventeen years old. That was not part of my life. When I was nineteen and was selected for the Walker Cup team, my focus shifted, but even

after that, golf was just one part of my life, and I tried not to let it dominate my every decision. For instance, once the kids were old enough, we took them bicycling, fishing, hunting, hiking, scuba diving, skiing, you name it. We did a lot of things together as a family. I never worried about how, say, my skiing with my kids was going to affect what I did on a golf course, or whether or not I was going to get hurt. Same with basketball; up until I was in my late thirties, I played in a basketball league. I still play tennis and love to do so.

I believe that my diverse interests not only made me a better golfer, but they also helped me extend my career by keeping me fresh. Furthermore, when it was finally time for me to hang up my spikes, I didn't have to wonder what I would do with the time I had previously devoted to golf.

The 1956 Upper Arlington High School varsity basketball team. I'm in the center of the front row.

the significance of SPORTSMANSHIP

I LOVE GOLF AND ITS UNIQUE CHALLENGES, trying to work through them, and the satisfaction that comes with achieving positive results. I have an equal affection for the traditions of golf. The honor and integrity, the sportsmanship, have always meant a great deal to me. Also, the game of golf is about responsibility. You hit the shots; you alone are accountable for the score you shoot, for your actions and for assessing penalties.

I'm not sure there are many people more determined and competitive than I am. I'm proud of my record in golf, but I've also tried throughout my life to do things the right way. I think you have to credit my mother and father for that—particularly my dad, because he spent so much time with me, and drilled into me the importance of sportsmanship. My father wasn't the type of person to tolerate poor behavior of any sort, particularly by his determined and sometimes overzealous son. He only had to see me throw a golf club in anger once to say that that would be the last one I would ever throw, or else I wasn't going to be playing golf. He meant it, too, and I got the message.

The 1978 Sports Illustrated *Sportsman of the Year award.*

My father also was very clear about how you handle yourself in the heat of competition. Sure, you want to win, but you should never behave in a way that cheapens the contest. If you win, you should be humble and modest. If you lose, then lose gracefully. Shake the hand of the man who's beaten you and tell him congratulations—and *mean* it.

My good friend Gary Player, as eloquent a public speaker as any person I've ever met, has been apt to say that I was not only the best winner in my day, but also the best loser, which implies I was adept at losing. I've asked Gary to substitute the word "gracious" for "best," or just say, "Jack is a good sport," but he won't do it. He gets a kick out of complimenting and teasing me at the same time.

Still, the bottom line here is that if you are going to compete in golf, you're going to have to get used to your share of disappointment. There isn't a player in the game who has ever won more tournaments than he lost. You put a hundred or more great players on the same golf course in a week, as you get at a major championship, and the odds just aren't in your favor. But that's part of the allure and challenge.

The hardest thing about sports is not acquiring the necessary skills to improve, whatever the level of competition. That takes work and commitment, but it can be done if you have the proper drive. No, the hardest thing is accepting with equal temperament the good and the bad. I learned long ago it's also the most important thing.

Although I didn't win the tournament, my dad looked awfully proud after my first U.S. Junior Amateur Championship.

1962: U.S. OPEN CHAMPIONSHIP

THE 1962 U.S. OPEN IN OAKMONT, Pennsylvania, was incredibly meaningful for me, well beyond the fact that it was my first professional victory, and that it gave me a lifetime exemption on the PGA Tour, which was a great relief to a rookie player. But I can remember several things that happened that week at Oakmont Country Club that shaped parts of my life significantly.

Obviously, of the utmost importance was winning that championship against Arnold Palmer near his hometown of Latrobe, Pennsylvania, with a highly pro-Arnold crowd around us. I knew that Arnold was my main competition; he was the man to beat at the time, and the confidence that came from that victory in a hard-fought playoff was significant. Obviously, this is the event where Arnold and I began our rivalry, and although the crowds that week were generally polite, their allegiance was clear. This never bothered me; I walked around with blinders on and didn't really pay much attention to the gallery. Arnold couldn't have been more of a gentleman as we

These tickets to the 1962 U.S. Open are reminders of how that victory immediately included me among the world's elite golfers.

played the first two rounds of the championship together—the U.S. Golf Association decided to play the entire championship in twosomes because of the severity of the layout—and then, of course, again in the playoff.

That playoff was something that even to this day remains vivid in my mind. I birdied the first couple of holes, and that was one great way to get started out at Oakmont. I remember Arnold coming down to the eighteenth, and that's the only time I ever saw him get disheartened. He drove it in the fairway, but he hit a fat 3-iron, and he looked like he knew it was over because from there he made a double bogey. I drove it just in the edge of the rough, and I'll never forget that Chick Hearn was the television announcer. I had taken out my wedge after Arnold's approach came up short, and I pitched my ball out into the fairway in front of a cross-bunker that was located about a hundred yards short of the green. I will always remember Chick's comment

The 1962 U.S. Open trophy is almost as bright as Barbara's smile. Above: Arnold and I were paired together for the first two rounds of the tournament.

after that shot. He said, "Oh my, gosh, he's choked." I said to myself, "You've got to be kidding; that's the first smart play I made all day." I knocked it on the green from there with a 9-iron and won the golf tournament.

I know that Oakmont was a golf course that I enjoyed playing, and I found it one of the best examples from the penal school of golf course architecture. I liked the difficulty of the greens and their extreme speeds, and although I already had a healthy appreciation and respect for the way the U.S. Golf Association set up its championship venues, I grew to have even more after that week. The '62 Open also was the tournament where I began the practice of visiting major venues the week prior to the championship. I had done this on the spur of the moment, flying over to Oakmont from Columbus. Seeing the course beforehand and having a sense of what kind of challenge awaited were beneficial to my preparation and understanding of what it would take to win. I think this ritual served me well over the years.

That tournament definitely had a significant impact on my image, or appearance, if you will, and my awareness for being a potential role model. I remember the thirteenth hole in the playoff with Arnold was the reason I quit smoking on the golf course. I remember I got the film of the Open later that year, on December 8. That's when we used to have a big reel film projector, and I put it on the reel at home and I sat down and watched it. I didn't like what I saw—and it had nothing to do with my golf. I watched as I lined up about a twenty-five-foot putt on the thirteenth, a par-three. I hit it up to the hole, and then I reached down on the ground and picked up my cigarette, and as I had it hanging out of my mouth, I went and tapped in the putt. I looked at that and said to myself, "Now that's the worst example for youth that I could ever imagine." Never mind how bad it looked in general.

I never smoked another cigarette on a golf course again. And even though I smoked for another fifteen years, maybe, I was really only a recreational smoker, and I started picking my places where I would smoke, if I was going to smoke at all. I wouldn't do it around my kids, I wouldn't smoke at home, and I wouldn't smoke in the office.

While the gallery was polite, there was little doubt where their allegiance rested.

Finally, the 1962 Open was a prelude to the development of my mutually respectful relationship with the media. The following year, in defense of my Open title at The Country Club in Brookline, Massachusetts, I shot a dismal 76–77 and missed the cut. Not only was I embarrassed by this, I was quite angry with myself. I was asked to go into the interview room to discuss my early exit from the championship, and I obliged. Again, I have my dad to thank for that, because he was clear about adhering to the responsibilities that go with being a professional athlete, and one of them was dealing with the media. I spent a good deal of time that day answering every question as honestly as I could, and I must have made an impression, because the assembled writers gave me an ovation when it was over.

It has been my practice ever since then to approach every interview request the same way, regardless of whether I play well or poorly. Whether I'm asked to conduct a press conference at a

I simply recognized that the media has a job to do, they have questions that need answers, and it's my responsibility to be as accommodating as possible.

major championship or whether a single writer wants a moment after a round, I've tried to make myself available, and to answer every question as thoroughly and honestly as I can. Sometimes, my honesty got me in a little trouble or ruffled some feathers, but that was never my intention. I simply recognized that the media has a job to do, they have questions that need answers, and it's my responsibility to be as accommodating as possible.

With few exceptions, I would say that because of this attitude, I've been treated by the media fairly well throughout the years. I don't think I have received preferential treatment, nor do I believe I ever should. But because I have exhibited respect for members of the media, they've given me a fair shake in return, which is all I could ever ask for.

the UNITED STATES OPEN CHAMPIONSHIP

I PLAYED IN MY FIRST UNITED STATES OPEN CHAMPIONSHIP AT INVERNESS GOLF CLUB IN TOLEDO, Ohio, in 1957, when I was seventeen years old. I played my last in 2000 at Pebble Beach Golf Links when I was sixty. I never missed America's national open golf tournament in that span, a run of forty-four straight years. When you do anything for forty years, it tends to become a part of you, and I feel that my relationship with the U.S. Open was a big part of my life, and a very special part of it, too.

Of the four major championships, the U.S. Open has been probably the most important to me simply because, first of all, it was the national championship of my home country. I also believe that because the Open is always conducted on great golf courses, and because of the way the U.S. Golf Association sets up those courses—with heavy rough bordering narrow fairways, firm conditions and fast greens—it is the most difficult of the four majors to win. It is pure, straight golf with an objective of identifying the best player, the one with patience, precision, course management, and good shot-making.

To win the U.S. Open four times, in 1962, '67, '72, and '80, is among the most satisfying experiences in my career. Because to me, the U.S. Open is a complete examination of a golfer. The

I saved this pin flag from the 1997 U.S. Open, which marked consecutive major championship number 150.

competition, what it does to you inside, how hard it is to work at, how hard it is to make it happen when the conditions aren't your ideal conditions—you have to persevere. I enjoyed that. I enjoyed the punishment, if that's what you want to call it. To grind that out and make a score at a U.S. Open makes you feel proud.

The U.S. Open—which usually ends on Father's Day, a circumstance I enjoyed and which my kids seemed to like—probably does more to make a man out of you than any other tournament.

You just never know what's going to happen to you at a U.S. Open, even when you know what the conditions and the challenges are going to be. You might shoot some 65s, which I did, including the final round of the 1967 U.S Open at Baltusrol to set the tournament record, but you might shoot some high scores, too, like the 82 in my final round at Pebble Beach in 2000, when fog suspended the first round after nine holes. What I shot that day was the best I could do; I tried on every shot. But Pebble Beach, my favorite golf course and where I won the '72 Open, wasn't in a friendly mood to me that day. That's the U.S. Open: If you're just not quite on your game, it eats you alive every time.

That was the aura and the beauty of the U.S. Open. That was the purity and simplicity of it. When you play in a U.S. Open, you know where you stand as a golfer.

There was plenty of golf between my first U.S. Open, in 1957 (left), and my last, in 2000, at Pebble Beach.

ENDORSEMENTS

I TALKED EARLIER ABOUT THE DISPARITY IN PRIZE MONEY TODAY COMPARED TO MY PEAK EARNING YEARS. I knew from the day I turned professional that I was never going to make a living strictly from golf tournament winnings. In the old days, outside pursuits comprised the bulk of a player's income. Exhibitions were one option. In fact, my first competitive paycheck after I turned professional came from a televised golf exhibition with Sam Snead, Arnold Palmer, and Gary Player, in Miami on the second-to-last day of 1961.

Endorsements, of course, were another avenue, and although I enjoyed many business relationships over the years, I never tried to go overboard and just sign on with anybody who came to me with a product to sell and a check in hand. Particularly in the 1970s, there were a lot of offers that came flooding in, but my business team and I tried to be selective. We sought relationships with outstanding companies that marketed top-line goods and services, and I always made sure

Advertisements for Jack Nicklaus Sportswear (above) and Brunswick Sports.

that I personally believed in the quality of the things I promoted. There were side benefits to limiting my commitments, namely maintaining my credibility as a spokesman and not spreading myself too thin with commitments of time and energy.

Even taking a minimalist approach to endorsements, I still made plenty of television commercials over the years and posed for countless print ads. Acting in commercials wasn't really my bag, but Barbara was a natural in front of the camera, and her performances pushed me to keep up with her. I'd have to say the commercials where we were able to get the whole fam-

ily involved were my favorites, like the skiing commercial for American Express. We did a lot of laughing behind the scenes.

I've enjoyed that part of my career, but I took it seriously, too. I have always insisted upon personally approving any text or graphics on print ads, or the scripts of TV commercials. I always felt that if you were going to do something, you should give it your full attention and effort. That was only fair to the companies who wanted me to be their pitchman.

my honorary degree from ST. ANDREWS

THE 1984 BRITISH OPEN AT ST. ANDREWS WASN'T ONE OF MY BEST PERFORMANCES, but it is still memorable for what happened early in the week, when I became the first sportsman in history to receive an Honorary Doctorate of Laws at the University of St. Andrews, Scotland's oldest educational establishment and one of the world's most renowned institutions of higher learning. This was quite a thrill, eclipsing another tremendous honor that I received in 1972, when Ohio State University granted me an honorary degree, a Doctorate in Athletic Arts. Jesse Owens, in the same ceremony, received a similar degree.

On Tuesday of championship week, I had to deliver an acceptance speech that may have been harder than any putt I ever sized up on the Old Course. Dressed in a black gown and white

The honorary degree from the University of St. Andrews in 1984 was deeply humbling. My acceptance speech (right) is one of only two I've written in advance.

tie, I faced an audience in the collegiate hall consisting of esteemed academicians and intellectuals, and I certainly felt the pressure of wanting to make a speech that conveyed my deep appreciation for such a prestigious honor.

The speech I gave at St. Andrews was one of only two I've ever written in advance—and I have had to give hundreds of speeches in my career. I know enough about myself to understand that I tend to do better when I'm working off the cuff and the things I say are simply coming from the heart. But some occasions are too big and too emotional, and I knew that any attempt to come up with the proper words off the top of my head would fail,

Speech to be delivered by Mr Jack Nicklaus at Graduation Ceremony at St. Andrews University on July 17

Vice-Chancellor, Mr McDowall, My Lords, Ladies and Gentlemen, Faculty and Students,

I am not a person who lives much in the past, but at a time like this, it is impossible to stop the mind from overflowing with special memories. If I were to try to share with you all of those, we would be here until well into the Open Championship, which would definitely not please your neighbors across the way at the Royal & Ancient. So I am going to limit myself to just a few remarks. Please do not mistake this brevity for lack of feeling or appreciation, because I assure you that what I have to say comes from my heart.

I am deeply honored to stand before you today for many reasons, but most of all as an individual who truly appreciates the close ties between my country and St. Andrews. This close relationship extends back to James Wilson, a native son of St. Andrews and a former student at this University, who signed our Declaration of Independence. But the link that means the most to me is the close tie that was developed between the University of St. Andrews and Robert Tyre Jones, Jr., a very special person in my life and an inspiration to all who had an opportunity to know him. I am extremely proud to be a Director of the Robert T. Jones, Jr. Memorial Scholarship Fund established in this fine man's name to honor both his tremendous contributions to golf and to the goodwill he built between our countries. It is a pleasure for me to salute the four 1984 Jones Scholars who are present here today.

I am particularly honored to be here at one of the world's most renowned universities. My participation in Higher Education came through one of America's largest universities, Ohio State. In retrospect, I learned many things at Ohio State, the chief among them being the great importance of institutions such as yours, not only in educating young people, but in helping them to achieve complete and fruitful lives as

only because I cared so much. The occasion in 1984, when I received that honorary degree, gave me yet one more reason to love that "Auld Grey Toon," as it is widely known.

The other written speech was at the 2000 Memorial Tournament, when the Captains Club chose me as that year's honoree during my final season playing all four major championships. To have my name added to the list of those we had honored in the game, a tradition that I was a part of initiating, well, you can't imagine how overwhelming that was. I get choked up thinking about it to this day.

TOM WATSON *and the* 1977 BRITISH OPEN

RESPECT AND ADMIRATION GO A LONG WAY IN THIS WORLD. It paves the way to friendships that, on the surface, couldn't seem possible. Growing up I didn't encounter many people who were as competitive as I was, but throughout my professional career, I ran up against some tough competitors, guys who wanted to beat me as badly as I wanted to beat them. You wouldn't think such an environment would foster friendships, but I've been lucky over the years to become friends with many of my strongest foes. How could that happen? Simple: mutual respect and admiration, plus a sense of camaraderie that golf inspires and the congeniality among contestants that cuts to the heart of the gentleman's game.

And, remember, it is only a game.

I've already talked about the special relationship I've enjoyed with Arnold Palmer and Gary Player. New challengers rose up time and again, like Lee Trevino, Ray Floyd, Johnny Miller, and

My scorecard from the 1977 British Open includes the yardages I'd marked for each hole.

Greg Norman, to name a few. We knocked heads plenty of times on the golf course, and I'll admit I believe their talent and level of play did nothing but spur me on to keep working and becoming a better player. However, we never let what happened on the course compromise a friendship, and I'm proud to call all those gentlemen my friends.

Trevino tended to give me the most fits, getting the better of me a couple of times in major tournaments, but no player dealt me a more significant series of emotional blows than Tom Watson did. And yet, I consider Watson, who is nearly ten years younger than I am, to be one of my closest friends. We've played a lot of practice rounds together, and we got along quite well as partners in various two-man competitions, including some Ryder Cup matches, where we were never beaten. As the years have passed and we stopped trying to beat each other's brains in, we've gotten even closer, and we have shared a few special moments in the last decade.

Tom and Luke Donald, a very talented and earnest youngster from England who I like very much, were my playing partners last year during the first two rounds of my final major championship, the British Open at St. Andrews. A popular player in his own right in Scotland, as much for his adherence to tradition and his gentlemanly manner as for his five British Open titles, Tom also joined me for a few practice rounds, and he understood what the week meant for me. Having Tom beside me on that occasion couldn't have been more fitting, and walking together up to the final green is one more terrific memory we share.

When Tom won the Memorial Tournament in 1996, his second victory at Muirfield Village Golf Club, I think I enjoyed that almost as much as the two wins I had there. To watch him come down the stretch and win at my tournament was a thrill for me. After walking off the eighteenth green with a two-shot victory, he walked straight toward me and we shared a hug. Tom's game had been awfully good for a long time, but until that triumph he hadn't won in nine years. You bet I was happy for him.

I'll admit I wasn't very happy with the results of some of his other victories, namely the ones where Jack William Nicklaus was the victim of his fine play. The 1977 Masters probably marked Tom's rise to the top of the game, and I believe that's where he supplanted me as the man to beat at the major championships. Though he is much more reserved than I am, Tom reminded me a lot of myself with his determination, his confidence, and his single-minded commitment to winning. Tom has a strong mind and always had a strong work ethic. Though his magnificent short game was his calling card, I knew he was an exceptional striker of the ball. In short, it was no surprise to me when he started asserting himself.

At the '77 Masters, Tom displayed the kind of course and pressure management that usually wins you the tournament. I played one of my finest final rounds to date, closing with a 66, but Tom just wouldn't crack. And when he birdied Augusta's seventeenth hole to take the lead, he forced me into the kind of mental error that I've always hated the most. Standing in the eighteenth fairway when the roar for his birdie erupted, I became a bit indecisive, hit a fat 6-iron, and lost by two strokes.

Even more deflating was his win, again by two shots, at the 1982 U.S. Open at Pebble Beach Golf Links. I thought I'd done everything necessary to win a record fifth Open title, shooting a final-round 69, highlighted by five straight birdies. My four-under-par 284 total was ten shots better than my winning aggregate total in the '72 Open at Pebble Beach. I was even surer of my chances when Watson flew his tee shot long and left over the green at the par-three seventeenth hole. Then he knocked his next shot into the hole, a chip that took luck, guts, and lots of skill—and still gets plenty of television airtime whenever the subject of great shots in major championships is discussed.

Of course, if there is one tournament that defines our playing rivalry, it has to be the 1977 British Open at Turnberry's Ailsa Course, in Ayrshire, Scotland. I played two of the greatest rounds of my life on the weekend—65–66—and posted my lowest aggregate score in a major championship, 269, to beat everyone by ten shots. This isn't mentioned much in the recaps, but if you scan the names filling out the top ten on the leaderboard, it's an impressive list: Hubert Green was third, Trevino fourth, Ben Crenshaw fifth, Palmer seventh, Floyd eighth, and Johnny Miller tied for ninth.

And Watson? Well, like I said, I beat everyone—everyone except Tom, that is, who shot 65-65 and nipped me by a stroke. It was by far the most thrilling head-to-head battle I'd ever been involved in. The two of us saw eye-to-eye on that issue as the final round unfolded. I caught his glance as we waited on the fourteenth tee, and he said to me, "This is what it's all about, isn't it

Jack?" I couldn't have said it better myself, so I simply replied, "You bet it is."

I think that attitude served me well going forward, especially since I was in the midst of a particularly frustrating period of major championship near misses. Since winning the 1975 PGA, I had finished second, third, or fourth in six of the next eight majors. But instead of folding up my tent, I simply went about my business, understanding that I had been on the winning end of many duels myself. I was rewarded for my perseverance by capturing the '78 British Open at St. Andrews, my second at the home of golf and third overall.

Last year, as I was cleaning out a closet at our home in Florida, I found an old glove smashed under a load of clutter. It was the glove from the final round of the '78 Open Championship, and I had signed and dated it: "7/15/78." I also found my contestant's badge from the tournament. Talk about a momentary flood of great memories.

One final postscript about Watson and the '77 Open: Tom paid me a tremendous compliment a few years ago when we conducted a joint interview prior to the 2003 Senior British Open at Turnberry and rehashed our "Duel in the Sun," as the media likes to refer to it. He said I helped him win because he was watching my swing and started copying it to some degree, and that got him into a good rhythm. I understood exactly what he was saying; I had done that plenty of times playing with Ben Hogan or Sam Snead or Julius Boros. I appreciated Tom saying that, and I guess that takes a little bit of the sting out of the setback all these years later—but not much.

Tom Watson was a determined competitor and true sportsman, and the 1977 British Open was a great battle to be a part of.

the GREEN JACKET

I WON MY FIRST MASTERS IN 1963, and the last of my six titles at Augusta National Golf Club more than twenty years ago. But I've owned one of the club's coveted green jackets for less than ten years.

I don't have nearly as much fun with this story as I did prior to 1998, when Jack Stephens, the former chairman of Augusta National, altered the punch line, but it still remains one of my favorites, and it never ceases to raise eyebrows among those in my audience whenever I get the chance to tell it.

As many readers might know, every Masters champion receives a green jacket and becomes a ceremonial, or honorary, member of the club. (Arnold Palmer and I in recent years were made full dues-paying members.) Ever since I first visited Augusta in 1959, when I was invited to play in the Masters as a member of the U.S. Walker Cup team, I have simply loved everything about it. To this day it remains one of my two most cherished places in golf, along with the Old Course at the Royal & Ancient Golf Club of St. Andrews, in Scotland. When I defeated the late Tony Lema

The Masters jacket pictured above is what every golfer wants to wear. In 1963, Arnold helped me into one that was a few sizes too large (right).

by one stroke to win the 1963 Masters Tournament, it was quite an emotional victory for me, especially given my special relationship with club founder, Bob Jones.

As the 1962 champion, it was Arnold's responsibility to help me slip on a green jacket at the awards ceremony—and I did the same for him when he won in '64, only to receive it again from Arnie in '65—but I didn't need a whole lot of help getting into that first coat, because the club had given Arnold a forty-six long to drape over me. And did it ever drape over me. It was like an overcoat; it was huge. To keep from looking kind of silly, I kept my elbows bent throughout the ceremony.

Now, the jacket wasn't for keeps. It was merely for show at the awards presentation, and club chairman Clifford Roberts later told me that the club would have a jacket made for me and ready upon my return the following spring. But when I arrived at Augusta for the '64 tournament, there was no jacket hanging in my locker in the Champions Locker Room. Not knowing quite what to do or say, I decided the best course of action was to simply borrow a jacket while I was on club grounds and not breathe a word to anyone. One that was available that year belonged to a man who was the former governor of New York, and who almost became president of the United States,

Thomas Dewey. He was the same Dewey who was the subject of the now infamous headline that appeared in the *Chicago Tribune* the day after the 1948 presidential election: "Dewey Defeats Truman." Right, that Thomas Dewey.

I wore Tom Dewey's jacket just about every year until it was practically worn out, and then in the early 1970s, I decided to have one made for me, though not by the Hamilton Tailoring Company, the Cincinnati-based company that has stitched the authentic single-vent coats for the club since 1967. I simply enlisted the help of clothier Hart, Schaffner & Marx, with whom I had an endorsement deal for many years. The jacket they made was fine by me, but it wasn't made of the same material, and it wasn't quite the same Kelly green shade as the official version.

I wore the Hart, Schaffner & Marx coat for about ten years, and then had to return to my borrowing ways. The jacket Bernhard Langer helped me into in 1986 was borrowed from someone, though I don't remember who. It fit nicely, though, I thought. You might think that I would have had a problem with this situation, but every year that went by, and each time I won at Augusta, the more I relished the irony of the situation. The public and the press thought I "owned" six green jackets. But only Barbara and I and a handful of people knew I didn't own any.

I mentioned 1998 as the year when Jack Stephens took some sting out of the punch line. I made the mistake of mentioning to Jack a few weeks before the tournament that I had won the Masters six times, but the club had never given me my own jacket. I said, "Do you think you could afford it?" Naturally, he was flabbergasted, and he demanded I go into the clubhouse immediately for a fitting. But I was hesitant. I told him it was a great story, and I didn't want to ruin it. That only delayed what ended up being inevitable. When I returned for the tournament, I found a note in my locker from Jack informing me that he had made a fitting appointment for me. That week I attended the traditional Champions Dinner for the first time in my own coat, a size forty-four regular.

I never needed my own jacket to feel like a part of the club, but it's nice to have one now that I am a full member. And if someone needs to borrow it, well, that's all right by me.

Bernhard Langer helps me into my sixth green jacket after the 1986 Masters.

the 1986 MASTERS

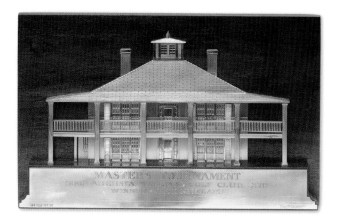

WHERE WOULD MY CAREER BE WITHOUT THE 1986 MASTERS? It's an interesting question, one that I fielded on numerous occasions as the twentieth anniversary of my final major championship victory arrived. Twenty years . . . it seems like yesterday—it really does. I can remember every club and yardage from the final round, the 65 I knew I had to have, just like I remember every detail of the 64 I shot in the third round of the 1965 Masters.

But the question about what the '86 Masters Tournament means to my career isn't easy to answer. Would I consider my career less satisfying or significant if I'd won seventeen professional majors instead of eighteen? Would the public's perception of my career be different? Would history's perception be different? I really can't say. I consider my sixth Masters victory the most fulfilling because it came at a time when not many people expected me to win, and I wasn't all that confident I could win either, although I never would have admitted it to anyone. What I will admit here is that I wasn't working on my game as diligently by then. I didn't prepare to the extent that I did when I was right in the middle of every major. I still thought about the Masters in January just like always, but the difference from my prime was that I didn't start working

My 1986 Masters trophy.

on it until about two weeks before the tournament—I'd always taken pride in preparing, and I always said there was no excuse for not being prepared. It should have been no surprise that I hadn't been playing well up to that point.

Rather than review for the umpteenth time the sequence of shots from that final round, not that I wouldn't enjoy it, I'd prefer sharing with you the things that make the memory of it so special. Undoubtedly, it was an exciting week for me and for the family. Having Jackie on the bag in his first Masters, the hug we shared at the end, that was great. I love the picture of the two of us walking off the eighteenth green arm in arm. I didn't give it much thought at the time, because I always hug my children. I still do. We also had my mother and my sister there. My mom hadn't

The '86 Masters added something to my career, obviously. I enjoyed a successful run up to that point, but I was clearly winding down.

been to the Masters since my first one in 1959, but she had undergone heart-bypass surgery the year before and maybe was feeling her oats, and she told my sister, Marilyn, she'd like to go to Augusta one more time. I remember there were so many people there that we rented a couple of houses and met every night for dinner in the main house, and I enjoyed that time with friends and family and relaxing every evening. There are just so many wonderful little stories—memories you never want to let go.

The '86 Masters added something to my career, obviously. I enjoyed a successful run up to that point, but I was clearly winding down. But something in me, probably just my stubborn ways, kept telling me I could still summon what I had back in my prime, and I could still use it coming down the stretch in a major championship. I may have been forty-six, but my nerves were still good. The fact that I then was able to summon what I needed to do down the stretch was very special to me, and I suppose it became special to the golf world in many ways, because they just didn't expect that to happen. I suppose it was an exclamation point on what, in hindsight, became truly the last year when I was competitive against players who were in their prime and

went on to have Hall-of-Fame careers, terrific players like Seve Ballesteros, Greg Norman, and Tom Kite—all who had a chance to win that Masters.

But I think the main difference the 1986 Masters made in my life was that twenty years later people want to keep talking about it, and it's the only one of my major championships that seems to resonate with people wherever I go. It's about the only event from the past where, when it comes on television, I actually stop and watch a little bit of it. And, I think to myself, "Yeah, I still made that putt. That was still a pretty good shot." But that's all. They're not going to change the film. I know how it ends. Just prior to the 2006 Masters, I was traveling for my design business and I turned on the TV in the hotel room and there was a clip of the '86 Masters. I looked at it for two minutes, went in and took a shower, and when I came out, the program had ended and they were replaying it again right on the heels of the last one.

I think the main difference the 1986 Masters made in my life was that twenty years later people want to keep talking about it.

Obviously, I knew the victory was going to have an impact on me—a positive one, of course—but it keeps having an impact, and it's flattering that it has stayed in everybody's mind. Maybe Tiger Woods has some influence on that, but maybe not. Most every time you pick up a newspaper today, Tiger is the subject when it comes to golf, and there's some relevance in regard to my record versus Tiger's, and that occasionally brings the '86 Masters into it. Still, it's a phenomenon that I can't fully comprehend. It's the only golf tournament that I can recall that everybody, when I see them, turns around and says, "Jack, '86 Masters, I was at a motel, or I was at an airport, or I was in this bar, or I was in this place and I couldn't leave, and my wife wanted to leave and I kept saying, 'No, no, no, we're not leaving until this is over.'" Thousands of people have told me that story. I've never heard those stories about any other golf tournament.

One of my fondest memories: Jackie and I share a hug after winning the '86 Masters.

TIGER WOODS

THE FIRST TIME I MET TIGER WOODS WAS IN CALIFORNIA. He was just a skinny kid with a name that you weren't going to forget and, even then, a swing that was impressive. I was at Bel-Air Country Club in Los Angeles for a reception, and I conducted a clinic for the members. During the clinic they brought this young kid out on the driving range. He might have been about thirteen years old. He came out and hit a few balls, and you could see that the talent was there.

Of course, it wasn't too long after that when Tiger started winning just about everything in sight. Before he turned thirty, he had collected ten major championships, more than halfway to my record of eighteen professional majors. He also accomplished something that I came within a stroke of doing myself, which was holding the trophies of all four majors simultaneously. Only a chip-in by Lee Trevino at the 1972 British Open at Muirfield, Scotland, prevented me from doing

I came into the interview room at Augusta and said I had just played with a kid who might win as many Masters as Arnold and I combined, which would be ten.

the same thing after I'd won the 1971 PGA Championship and the '72 Masters and U.S. Open, though I didn't win them consecutively.

I think the first time I spent a significant amount of time with Tiger was prior to the 1996 Masters, when Arnold and I played a practice round with him after he won the U.S. Amateur. Boy, were the two of us impressed with what that young man could do on the golf course. I came into the interview room at Augusta and said I had just played with a kid who might win as many Masters as Arnold and I combined, which would be ten. A lot of the media at the time

kind of scoffed at that, and, sure, I said it partly in jest. But Tiger is thirty years old and he's got

a good jump on getting there—four and counting. Ten years or so from now, I might be saying,

"I told you so."

Tiger has made no secret that his goal is to break all my records, primarily my record of

eighteen professional major championships. Naturally, as a way of generating stories, writers

ask me all the time who would win a battle between Tiger and me if we were both in our primes.

This isn't a new line of questioning, because writers have always wondered how the best from

different eras would stack up against one another. My answer has always been the same: Great

players would be great in any era. As for going against Tiger head-to-head, all I know for certain is

that he would be trying his hardest to beat me and I would be trying my hardest to beat him.

Arnold and I were immediately impressed when we played a round with Tiger Woods in 1996.

The other question that's always thrown at me relates to our similarities. I see a lot of similarities between us. He hits the ball farther, relatively speaking, than I did; perhaps equipment has something to do with that. However, his power game puts him in a position to win as often as my power game did for me, though neither of us uses power exclusively to try to win a tournament. Tiger manages his game well; I managed my game well. He's probably better playing right-to-left shots, but I played most of the time left-to-right, except on rare occasions, such as at Augusta. He has a far better short game than I ever had. He's a terrific putter, but I think I was a good putter,

Both of us had the experience of winning young, winning amateurs, and winning a Masters at a young age—learning how to win.

too. And I think he feels like if he's hitting the ball well, then he'd have to do something, make some kind of error, not to win the tournament he's in; I felt that way a lot of times. Both of us had the experience of winning young, winning amateurs, and winning a Masters at a young age—learning how to win. That's about as close as I can come on that analysis.

Can he beat my records? I believe he can. It might be a little more difficult now that I've stopped playing in major tournaments. Every time I came to a major for the last time, Tiger went out and won the tournament. So I've stopped helping him there. (I'm kidding, of course.)

His biggest problem is probably going to be whether he can keep his desire and interest to do it, plus he has to have a little bit of luck, like I did, health-wise. He'd already had knee and back problems before he was thirty. Only time will tell, but it sure appears to me that we haven't seen any wavering of determination or enthusiasm. To undertake the swing changes he made in the last few years, after the success he already had, was, I think, a good thing for him if it means helping him to stay healthy.

He's certainly blessed with a wealth of talent, he's got a fantastic work ethic, and he has a great desire to win. He doesn't play just for money; to be a great player you can't have money be a

Tiger and I share a laugh at the 2000 PGA Championship.

motivator. He's going to have to have discipline, which all champions have. Arnold Palmer had it, Ben Hogan had it, Byron Nelson had it. I think he has it; he's shown that so far. He came out into this golf world under a tremendous amount of expectation and pressure and performed, and he has performed at the highest level every single time he's teed it up. I think what he did in winning four major championships in a row was a phenomenal achievement.

He's got a much more difficult media run than I had. He's been under scrutiny and in the spotlight since he was five years old. You want to talk about pressure on this guy. He's had it ever since he was a youngster. You can go back and find film clips of when he was two. It's just an unbelievable story. Certainly he's got more competition than I had, though I would argue that although there are more good players today, there were more great players in my day.

I said this for a long time, and it's sort of a cliché: Records are meant to be broken. I think they are. In every sport somebody has come along to break somebody else's records. Mine might be difficult to break, but somebody is going to come along and do it, and if it's Tiger who does it, I couldn't have chosen a better candidate.

How would I feel about that? I'd love to see it happen. I would prefer to see it done in my lifetime rather than leave this world not knowing what was going to happen.

It was quite a privilege to give Tiger the Memorial Tournament trophy in 2000.

my DESIGN PHILOSOPHY

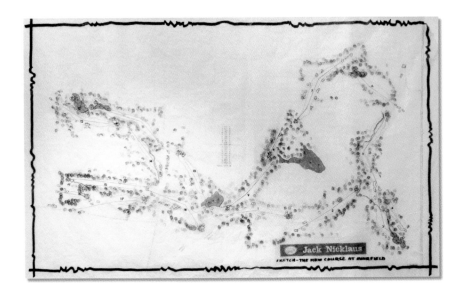

MY DESIGN PHILOSOPHY IS AS STRAIGHTFORWARD AS I AM. I simply try to design the best course that I can, to create one that is interesting, challenging, and beautiful, one that fits with the land I'm given, and one that meets the needs of the person who has asked me to design it. When I am given a piece of property, I take my most important cues from the person who hires me. I want to create a golf course that will fulfill the owner's needs, desires, and goals. When the golf course is completed, I evaluate my success in terms of whether I have met those criteria. My job is to turn their vision into a golf course. If the owner is happy when I am finished, then I feel we have been successful.

How I got started on what has become an enjoyable and fulfilling second career can be traced, as you might expect, to my playing career. Once I started playing all over the country and throughout the world, the exposure to new layouts—my guess is I've played about five hundred

My course designs generally start out as rough sketches, such as this one of Muirfield Village Golf Club.

golf courses—forced me to consider how I needed to play them strategically. After a period of time, I looked at them with an even more critical eye, seeing ways in which various layouts might be improved, and mentally redesigning certain holes.

In the mid-1960s, Pete Dye allowed me to get my feet wet in the architecture process, asking for my input in his design of The Golf Club in suburban Columbus, and that was a great experience. We later collaborated on a handful of other projects, including Harbour Town Golf Links on Hilton Head Island, South Carolina. I also worked with Desmond Muirhead on several courses, and his land planning was helpful in my design of Muirfield Village Golf Club. Finally, I got to the point where I wanted to have my own expression, and my first solo effort opened in 1976 at

Course designs require a lot of site visits, such as this one at Harbour Town, with Pete Dye (right).

Glen Abbey, in Toronto, Canada, which has been a regular host site for the Canadian Open. Later that year, in Alabama, I completed my first solo project in the United States, Shoal Creek.

One of the reasons I got involved in golf course design at a fairly young age was because it was something else that kept me in the game and challenged me, but for about ten or twelve years it was mostly a hobby. An expensive one, as it turned out, so then I turned it into a business. I'm proud to say it's been a very healthy business, too, with Nicklaus Design topping three hundred

One thing that I have always tried to keep in mind is that the game is meant to be fun. Another is my belief that golf is a game of precision more than strength.

courses around the world (in twenty-eight countries) by the middle of 2006, and me having a hand in more than two hundred and fifty of those designs.

Evolution is part of any golf course, and there's been an evolution in my design skills over the years. There was some early criticism of my work, but instead of letting it bother me, I took it to heart. I listened to what others had to say, and tried to learn from that and do better. In my early golf courses, I tended to look more at shots, and saw a lot of left-to-right shots because that is how I played golf. Today, I don't look at it as a shot being played. I look first at what the land is and how I can best make the course fit into the land, because the surrounding environment helps determine the overall character of the golf course and of each hole. Before, I would fit the golf course to the shot. You can't force an idea on a piece of land.

One thing that I have always tried to keep in mind is that the game is meant to be fun. Another is my belief that golf is a game of precision more than strength. It's a thinking person's game. There's no challenge in just whacking the ball. A golf course should be enjoyable and offer variety to every golfer, no matter what his or her level of skill or strength. My primary aim is to test a golfer's accuracy. I try to use the richest possible mix of shot values—varied tests of precision.

Are there any trademarks to Jack Nicklaus-designed courses? Not really. I always strive for excellence in my designs, but I try to avoid using features that might be tagged as distinctive "trademarks." If the natural attributes of a hole suggest it, I might use a strategy or concept similar to what I have employed elsewhere, but I will strive to make it unique in appearance; there are plenty of sound principles you can use to change the look of a hole, and options include water, dunes, trees, size of bunkers and greens, or widths of fairways. But, again, it all has to mesh with the environment.

These days I'm busier than I've ever been because of my design business, and I love every minute of it. Having my kids involved is a true bonus. I don't think I ever put five hundred hours on my airplane, Air Bear, as a touring pro, but I'll certainly put over five hundred hours on the airplane this year doing golf course work.

Through the years there have been more than five hundred professional tournaments staged on courses that we have designed. It's nice to look back and see things like that, and it's a tremendously nice compliment. There's no feeling like walking up the eighteenth fairway at a major, but the satisfaction I get in designing a golf course is a close second.

The plans I'm holding in this 1972 picture would transform the setting into Muirfield Village Golf Club two years later.

golf course ARCHITECTURE

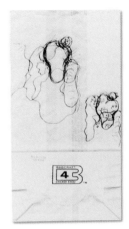

YOU NEVER KNOW WHEN AN IDEA IS GOING TO STRIKE, and I've always found it better to put it down somewhere so that the people you are working with understand your vision of a particular part of a golf course. When I'm out in the field, I'm always making adjustments. It's part of my routine when I visit a site. What I've discovered over time is how much people enjoy them, so my design company has made it a practice to take all of my sketches from a particular project and give them to the club when the course is completed. Many times I've scribbled on the other side of the routing plans, or right over top of the hole renderings, so the alterations are as clear as I can make them. It could be a greens complex or a bunker shape; I draw it all out when I want to show what I want to see accomplished before my next visit. Sometimes I wonder if I'm the only one who understands these sketches, though most of my design guys have developed a knack for deciphering them. I have a great team, that's for sure.

Now, when a golf course is finished, we encourage clubs to hold on to the sketches, put them in a frame, and display them. It's sort of a nice commemorative gesture. These

These sketches for The Bear's Club in Jupiter, Florida, were drawn on a napkin (left) and a paper bag.

I think one of the most intriguing aspects to golf course architecture has been the mental exercise required to bring a golf course from conception, through all the stages, to a finished product.

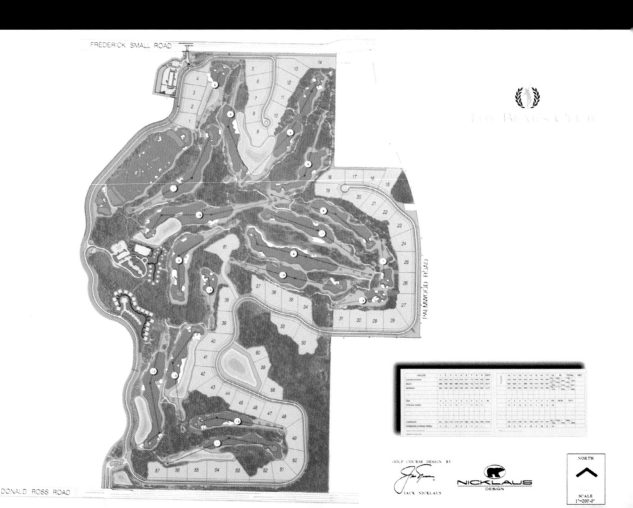

are very primitive sketches, obviously. I'm not completely certain why people like them, but it's very flattering.

I think one of the most intriguing aspects to golf course architecture has been the mental exercise required to bring a golf course from conception, through all the stages, to a finished product.

Obviously, the challenge is intrinsically different from playing the game and competing in championship golf. But in some ways it is more demanding, and I could just as easily argue that there is more pressure inherent in golf course design. A wayward shot can be quickly forgotten—at least that's the goal if you intend to have success competing—and its resulting problems can be corrected with the next stroke. One wrong move in building a course isn't nearly as easy to fix. Furthermore, though a bad stroke can cost you a tournament and quite a bit of money, a poor design decision could cost one of your clients millions of dollars. Put in those terms, you can see that the design business, though it's something I thoroughly enjoy, can have its own sources of immense pressure. Of course, the fact that it is so thoroughly challenging is one of the reasons I have found it so much fun.

I like to think that I put a lot of myself into every one of the courses I design. My hope is that people will see that, appreciate what I have tried to do in my design career, and enjoy playing the golf courses as much as I enjoyed designing them. My golf game, obviously, has run its course. I had my time. But what I have learned all these years I can still put into a piece of ground, and that will last beyond me or my records.

There's a great sense of accomplishment when I see the final design, like this one for The Bear's Club.

the "GOLDEN" POLAR BEAR

WE HAVE A GIANT POLAR BEAR ON DISPLAY JUST OUTSIDE THE MEN'S LOCKER ROOM AT THE BEAR'S CLUB, the private club I built near my home in Florida, and some people make the mistaken assumption that it's a prize from one of the many hunting trips I've taken over the years.

The truth is, it's actually a gift from a man I never met in person.

In 1986, I was playing in the PGA Grand Slam of Golf at Kemper Lakes Golf Club, near Chicago, with the other major-championship winners from that year—Raymond Floyd, Greg Norman and Bob Tway. As I was walking down the fifteenth fairway, a young lady ran under the ropes toward

This present from a fan is probably the only polar bear in South Florida.

me, which made me and everyone else around us a little uneasy at first. But then she threw her arms around me and began to cry. She said, "Jack, my father is dying of cancer. He is such a fan of yours. Would you do me a big favor and call him?" My answer was, "I can't right now. But I would be happy to talk with him after the round is completed."

She met me after the round, and we called her father, who happened to be a doctor, Walter J. Murawski. After a few moments he said to me, "Jack, I know I sound fine, but I only have a few months to live." He went on to tell me that he had taken a polar bear in Alaska, and at the time,

---

He went on to tell me that he had taken a polar bear in Alaska, and at the time, it was said to be the fourth largest ever taken.

---

it was said to be the fourth largest ever taken. He added, "The bear has a golden hue, and it has always reminded me of you. I have been a great fan of yours, and when I pass away, I would like for you to have the bear as a gift from me." I told him how much I appreciated his nice gesture, and I assured him that I would find a good home for his "golden" polar bear.

At the time, we were building Wynstone Golf Club, which is near Chicago, and we decided to place the bear there. For about ten years the bear was housed just outside the pro shop in the Wynstone clubhouse.

When my dream of The Bear's Club became a reality, it seemed appropriate to me that the polar bear's home should be in South Florida, because there could be no better place than The Bear's Club to remember such a devoted fan.

AWARDS

THE WAY I FEEL ABOUT AWARDS IS VERY DIFFERENT FROM HOW I FEEL ABOUT TROPHIES. When I go out and win a golf tournament, that's something I did on my own; it's an accomplishment, and it's a rewarding experience. In some ways, however, receiving an award is even more special.

Sometimes my success on the golf course led to certain honors, such as the Golfer of the Century award I received in 1988 at the "Centennial of Golf in America Celebration," or *Sports Illustrated*'s Individual Male Athlete of the Century award. Those are monumental when you think about all the great players or athletes who would have been considered. Just being in the company of such people is overwhelming in itself, and I get emotional when I think about the times I've been recognized.

Every award I've received I look at the same way: I'm humbled. Everybody likes to be honored and everybody likes to be recognized. And when people go out of their way to say "thank you" and "nice going," I get very sentimental.

I really don't care if the award is presented to me on national television or in front of fifty people. If somebody thinks enough of you and the things you've accomplished to want to recognize you in some way, well, how could you ever treat that with a flip?

The bronze statue that was given to me in 1988 for Golfer of the Century now greets visitors to the Jack Nicklaus Museum. Originally the statue came with me swinging an iron. I had it switched to a driver. It just seemed more appropriate.

What's important to note is not what I received, but the trouble that people went through to give me something so special and memorable.

I received the Golfer of the Century award in 1988, quite a humbling experience. The statue now greets visitors to the Jack Nicklaus Museum.

the importance of FITNESS

THROUGH THE YEARS, I've been very lucky because I've been healthy for much of my career. I have had to withdraw from only two tournaments because of injuries—the 1981 World Series of Golf before the fourth round, and the 1983 Masters after the first round. I don't think you can play in 154 straight majors without having more than a little bit of luck, but I've also taken pretty good care of myself—and certainly benefited from having such a great wife like Barbara around when I occasionally get off track, mostly in regard to my diet. I'm very proud of my longevity, and I think that longevity speaks to the fact that I've worked pretty hard.

I've also been fairly disciplined throughout the years. I have tried to make intelligent choices about my health. After the 1969 Ryder Cup, I realized that it was probably time for me to lose some weight, and I was able to drop twenty pounds in preparation for the 1970 season without noticing any discernable loss of power. I was a recreational smoker, but I eventually decided that I needed to stop in my mid-thirties, and did so cold turkey. And not many people know this, but I haven't touched a soft drink since 1989.

Another streak I'm pretty proud of is never missing a day of stretching and exercise since Thanksgiving, 1988. That's when Pete Egoscue, a functional anatomist and a good friend, began tailoring workouts for me to address the inevitable physical problems that come with age and the years of wear and tear associated with golf.

I think the first time I started making adjustments for age was when I was about nineteen, and I've been making them ever since. Some of those adjustments have been a little more serious than others, but honestly, that's when I first started to notice little problems cropping up here and

Overcoming a third-round 73 to win the 1975 Masters was one of my most thrilling victories.

there. I won tournaments where I hurt myself in the morning, or hurt myself sleeping, or had a sore neck. I remember the first time I won the Crosby, now called the AT&T Pebble Beach National Pro-Am. I got up in the morning and I was doing some stretches, and my back started to go into spasms. I couldn't move my left side, I couldn't do anything with it—and I'm a left-to-right player. I need my left side to be strong to be able to play against it. I almost withdrew, but then I figured, well, I can hit hooks. So, I just aimed to the right and started playing hooks, and I shot 37 on the front nine, and I came back and shot 31 on the back nine playing that way.

That was a bit extreme, but the point is you have to play with what you've got. But in later years, to make sure that I minimized those types of problems, I've worked out every day—and sometimes twice a day—for over six thousand straight days, and that includes the day I had my hip replacement surgery in January 1999. I have to think the regimen I stuck to allowed me to return to competitive golf faster than expected. It also allowed me to dance at my son's wedding. Michael got married about three weeks after the hip surgery, and I was able, with the help of crutches, to do a little four-legged two-step, as I would call it, with Barbara.

I think the first time I started making adjustments for age was when I was about nineteen, and I've been making them ever since.

Pete's workouts have allowed me to eliminate dysfunctional areas, most notably ruptured discs in my back, and avoid having surgery for many years. I finally had to have a minor surgical procedure in 2004 for stenosis, a narrowing of the area around the spinal cord that was causing pain and weakness in my legs; that was something I couldn't work my way out of. But through diligence and my own stubbornness, I've been able to stretch and pull and exercise my way out of a lot of troubles, and that's why I still have the ability to physically do things that I enjoy doing.

the GOLF BALL

I'VE BEEN TALKING ABOUT THE GOLF BALL—specifically the increasing distances that balls keep going—for close to twenty-five years. Advancing technology in golf balls enabled me to remain somewhat competitive beyond the time I probably should have been. I used a Callaway HX Tour ball at my last Masters and at my last British Open. I may have my objections to the way the golf ball is affecting the game, but if I was going to continue to play, I had to find a ball that would give me a reasonable chance to compete against the likes of Tiger Woods and Ernie Els. After all, I'm not crazy.

Another advantage a player gains with today's golf balls is that they not only stay in the air longer, but they also fly straighter. In my last few competitive seasons I didn't work on my game that much, and predictably, I made my share of poor swings. I can't tell you how many times I looked up after what I thought wasn't my best swing and the ball was going straight. How did that happen?

This is light years ahead of where we were in my prime. Back in 2000, I remember Frank Thomas telling me about that old Tourney ball I was playing, the type I used for much of my career. Frank was the technical director for the United States Golf Association at the time, and he was responsible for testing new equipment so that it conformed to the Rules of Golf. Well, Frank told me prior to my last U.S. Open at Pebble Beach that he tested those old golf balls, and

Above is the ball used in what is likely the final Masters hole of my career, in 2005.

one went twenty yards shorter than the previous one, another went twenty yards to the right, and one twenty yards left. "How you could win tournaments with that golf ball, I don't ever know," he said. "It has to be one of the worst balls ever made."

Today, there's not a manufacturer out there who can't make a high-quality golf ball that just goes forever. In the last five years or so, the leap in technology has been incredible, especially when you factor in other advances, such as matching up a certain club with a ball to dial in launch angles and the fact that golfers, like other athletes, are getting bigger and stronger, and we're seeing a distance revolution that not only is changing the intrinsic nature of the game but also is creating an ever-widening gap between the recreational golfer and the world's top players.

Technology today has become a good player's technology. It started out to be an average golfer's technology, with player-improvement clubs and so forth, but equipment manufacturers have taken the technology over the top to where the game really helps the pros, helps the big hitter, but it doesn't help the average golfer significantly. You put together a high-tech ball and a high-tech driver and put it in the hands of a top professional who hits the ball in the rear end every time, and you'll see drives consistently three hundred yards or more. The average golfer hits it in the rear end maybe one out of ten times or one out of twenty times, and when they do, they say, "Oh, look how far that ball goes." But the other nineteen times they lose about fifty yards. How do you learn how to play with fifty yards of difference between a good shot and a bad shot? We didn't used to have that.

I think the game is much harder now for the average golfer. Today's equipment might help them hit a few more good shots, but when they lack the consistency, it's awfully hard to shoot a decent score, which is why scoring averages for recreational golfers haven't improved much despite all this new equipment. That's a big concern of mine; I'm concerned about bringing people in the game and keeping them in the game. I've said over and over again that I don't think we can harness technology—and to a degree I don't think we should. But at the very highest levels, we should start to consider reining it in some, just because of how it's changing the game and what it's costing us.

I've long contended that to keep up with technology, we basically have to change every golf course in the world, because the game is different and you're applying a new game to old golf courses. We do this for one reason: because the golf ball is making old courses obsolete. Wouldn't it make more sense, wouldn't it be less expensive, to change the golf ball for tournament play? If we had started the game playing it this way, with power being almost everything, golf courses would be totally different. They'd all be 7,500 yards or so. Then one day we'd decide that land was way too valuable to keep building golf courses of that length, and we'd start building shorter golf courses, yet keep playing a ball that went far. That would be a problem. What would we do? I think it's obvious that we would change the golf ball.

This wouldn't be a hard thing to do at all, and probably not nearly as expensive as all the money we invest in research and development to design golf balls that can go farther. Each

If we had started the game playing it this way, with power being almost everything, golf courses would be totally different. They'd all be 7,500 yards or so.

manufacturer could roll back the distance of the ball 10 percent or 12 percent, or whatever it might be, and everyone would have to play that ball, but they could keep the characteristics that best suited their games. How long will it take a Tour-level player to get used to that? My estimate: two rounds of golf. How much time and money it would take to change every golf course that they play? A lot.

That's just my philosophy. Manufacturers won't agree with me, I'm pretty sure, but I think this is what has to be done. If I had my way, I would have done it twenty years ago, before every golf course in this country became obsolete. To have courses be diminished by a golf ball because the manufacturers can't stand to have their golf ball go shorter, and because the people at the USGA can't make a stand because they're concerned about being sued—and I don't blame them—where do you go? The game gets ruined, and that's not right.

9 - Birdies - 1 Eagle - 8 Pars - - 11 - 3's
1 - 2
8 - Pars
No Bogies

All putts Holed - Official Record. *Colin Holder*

Hole	Men's Course	Men's Par			Handicap	Strokes		+ 0	Ladies' Course	Ladies' Par
1	348	4	3	4	11	③	4	—	348	4
2	356	4	4	4	7	③	4	+1	356	4
3	350	4	4	4	9	4	4	+1	330	4
4	125	3	2	3	17	②	3	+1	125	3
5	370	4	4	4	5	③	4	+2	338	4
6	398	4	4	4	1	4	4	+2	362	5
7	297	4	4	4	13	③	4	+3	297	4
8	301	4	3	3	15	③	4	+3	301	4
9	379	4	4	3	3	4	4	+3	379	4
Out	2924	35	32	33		29	36		2836	36
10	200	3	3	3	18	3	3	+2	152	3
11	370	4	4	4	8	③	4	+3	324	4
12	460	5	5	4	4	③	4	+4	420	5
13	225	3	4	4	14	3	3	+5	204	3
14	431	4	4	4	2	4	4	+5	390	5
15	353	4	4	4	12	③	4	+6	353	4
16	349	4	4	4	10	4	4	+6	349	4
17	349	4	4	4	6	4	4	+6	349	4
18	347	4	5	4	16	③	3	+7	347	4
In	3084	35	37	36		36	38		2888	36
Tot.	6008	70	69	69		⑤⑨	74		5724	72
Handicap										
Net Score				All Time Course Record.						

PLAYER *Jack Nicklaus*

ATTEST *Colin Holder* DATE *Mar-12-73*

(Chairman)

There are two major factors changing the game, and the one you can't control is the size of the athlete. Golfers are getting to be bigger and better, just like athletes in every other sport. That leaves technology. If you are going to continue to let the golf ball improve for distance, then you're going to keep seeing classic courses like Augusta National Golf Club lengthening, doing whatever they can to stay ahead of the curve. I said a few years ago that pretty soon we'll be teeing off in the Masters in downtown Augusta somewhere. Hootie Johnson, who was chairman of the Masters and Augusta National Golf Club at that time, jokingly had a plaque installed on the eighteenth tee the next year that read, simply, "Downtown." Of course, since then they've gotten closer yet to downtown, with another 155 yards added to the course for the 2006 Masters.

Power is always an advantage in this game, always has been an advantage. I had that advantage in my day, but back then it was maybe fifteen to twenty yards. It's much more of an advantage today, and the advantage sometimes can be fifty yards or more between the long hitters and average-length players. It's a different game today, and it is a power game today; power makes up about 90 percent of how the outcome of a tournament is decided. Its importance has become too disproportionate to other parts of the game. From about the late 1930s or early 1940s to about '95, the game of golf didn't change very much at all. It changed some, but it was still basically played the same way.

Since then, it has changed dramatically. Do I like it? No. One reason is that it's very difficult to compare the game today with the game that I played, and guys who played in the generation prior to this one. Do I accept it because that's what it is? Yes, of course I do. But my feeling is you should still try to bring shot-making and strategy into the game as much as you can, because that is the heart of the game—and it always should be.

The ball used for my lowest round ever—a 59 at The Breakers in Palm Beach, Florida, in 1973—was quite a bit different than the balls used in today's tournaments.

the FIVE-POUND BANKNOTE

THE GOOD PEOPLE OF SCOTLAND HAVE BEEN VERY GRACIOUS TO ME OVER THE YEARS AND HAVE SORT OF TAKEN ME IN AS ONE OF THEIR OWN. I felt that way every time I returned for the British Open. Still, nothing could have prepared me for the wonderful gesture by The Royal Bank of Scotland when it issued currency with my likeness on it.

When Sir Fred Goodwin of RBS called me and asked me if it would be all right to do this, I was speechless. It was so flattering that RBS, in any way, shape or form, would think of me and honor me in this way.

It's incredibly overwhelming when you think that only two other living persons have appeared on a Scottish banknote, and both are royalty: Her Majesty, the Queen, and the late Queen Mother.

Obviously, I'm an American, not a Scot or a Brit, but RBS realized that St. Andrews and Scotland in general have been a special part of my life and my career, and they wanted to commemorate my last visit to the Open Championship. It's one of the most significant and memorable honors I've had in my career.

I'll say it again: I never played professional golf for the money. The fact that my likeness appears on currency is, I guess, what you'd call irony. In the end I'd still have to call it, above all else, quite humbling.

The Royal Bank of Scotland put into circulation two million five-pound notes with my likeness on them.

ST. ANDREWS

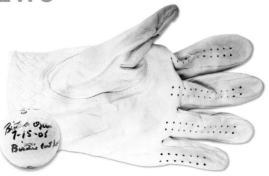

THERE COULD HAVE BEEN NO BETTER PLACE FOR ME TO END MY COMPETITIVE CAREER
THAN IN SCOTLAND, at the Old Course at St. Andrews. Augusta National Golf Club and St.
Andrews are two of my favorite places in golf, and it would have been just as appropriate for me
to stop at the Masters, but the order of the schedule being what it is, St. Andrews was my final
tournament, the last time that I would likely play as a golfer and a competitor.

I thought I had played my seventh and final time at St. Andrews, as well as my final British Open, in 2000. I fully expected 2000 to be my last time there, but at the Champions Dinner
in the clubhouse of the Royal & Ancient Golf Club, I was with Peter Dawson, secretary of the
R&A, and I asked him when the Open was coming to St. Andrews again. He said there hadn't
been an announcement yet, but the R&A was thinking about 2006. I said, "Oh, that's too bad,
I'll be sixty-six, past the age of eligibility." An exemption for past champions expires after age
sixty-five. Peter said, "That's right. If it happened to be 2005, would you come back?" Next thing
you know I read in the newspaper that the British Open was going back to St. Andrews in 2005.
I thought that was an awfully nice compliment. And if the R&A decided that they wanted to
make sure that their date was going to coincide with my sixty-fifth birthday, I thought that
was a nice honor. It would be a kick in the teeth to them if I didn't go back. Still, I wanted to

*It was wonderful going out with a birdie on the final hole of my last British Open in 2005, and perhaps the last major
championship of my career.*

go back as a golfer, not some kind of a monument. I wanted to go back while I still had some semblance of a game.

The Old Course is a very special place to me simply because of what it is, where it is, how it sits in the town, and how it relates to the history of the game of golf. Plus, the people have always treated me so wonderfully, as they have wherever the British Open has been held. I suppose if you took St. Andrews and put it somewhere else, it might be just another fine golf course. But because of where it is, because of what it has meant to the game of golf, because it's a public facility that is more a part of the town than a shrine, it becomes something extraordinary.

The Old Course is a very special place to me simply because of what it is, where it is, how it sits in the town, and how it relates to the history of the game of golf.

My personal history at St. Andrews also has plenty to do with how I feel about it. Again it starts with Bob Jones, who tore up his scorecard and stomped off St. Andrews the first time he played it, and then came back and won the British Open at the Old Course in 1926. Jones said your career is never complete as a great golfer unless you can win at St. Andrews. I always had that on my mind because I grew up knowing all there was to know about Jones.

But that's the way St. Andrews is. You can hate it and then love it. I mentioned how much my father disliked it when he played there in 1959, but when I first saw the Old Course in preparation for the '64 Open Championship, I went around and said to myself, "This place is great." I loved it, with those bunkers, and the names they have for them. I don't know all the names, but I can probably go around and name fifteen or twenty. You can't do that anywhere else. And then you have all the humps and bumps, and the double greens, which are very tough, and the shot values. I wasn't expecting anything, and I got so much more. It was different than anything I had ever played, and

The crowd gave me a wonderful ovation after that birdie on the final hole at St. Andrews.

it has stood the test of time with golfers from years and years ago, and never really has changed. We don't play any other golf course like this one. There's just no other golf course that is even remotely close. They've added yardage to it in recent years, like they have everywhere else, but it's basically the same golf course since I first visited it, and it's the only golf course I can think of that I have played exactly the same way, with the same clubs every time, including 2005.

St. Andrews always had a way of bringing out my best. When I won there in 1970, it ended a three-year drought in major championships, but the victory was so emotionally meaningful for me because I had lost my father earlier in the year, so I dedicated that win to him. Then I won again in 1978, after the disappointment of losing to Tom Watson at Turnberry the year prior, and again it ended a three-year major drought. I think the Open Championship in general brought out some of my best golf. The British Open is very different golf, and I enjoyed the break. The style of play required to win it was something that was not my forte, but I learned to adapt my game to it and deal with the elements and execute different shots. Those were the things that I always liked about going there.

The style of play required to win it was something that was not my forte, but I learned to adapt my game to it and deal with the elements and execute different shots.

Then you have the Scottish people, who treat all golfers so well; they embrace you and take you in as one of their own. I felt that same kind of affection again in 2005, and it was all a very emotional time for me. My exit came about too early, because I missed the cut, but that was OK. I did the best I could, and shooting 72, even par, for my last round was pretty decent for a guy just trying to get out of the way. And, of course, making a birdie on the last hole was one heck of a way to end it all. I wanted that putt very badly, but I knew that the hole would move wherever

The 1978 British Open victory was especially gratifying after losing at Turnberry the previous year.

I hit it. It always happens on the last hole; I just figured it would go in. So I hit it and it went in. I'm kidding, but it did seem like fate smiled on me there, as it did many times at St. Andrews.

I take a lot of great memories with me, with the reception from the gallery right at the top. I think that I've had the good fortune to receive many heartwarming receptions from fans through the years, but that was among about five that truly stand out. The first time I had the gallery react with so much excitement was at the '72 Open at Muirfield, when I won the first two majors and was far behind in the final round, then pulled myself back into the tournament. The gallery

The gallery reaction was wild. That was the first time I had ever been on a golf course and had tears on my face in the middle of a round.

reaction was wild. That was the first time I had ever been on a golf course and had tears on my face in the middle of a round. The second was '78 at St. Andrews, with people coming out of the rafters—that was unbelievable. Then there was the 1980 U.S. Open at Baltusrol. I hadn't won the year before and there I was on the way to tying Jones with my fourth U.S. Open victory. There were signs proclaiming, "Jack's back," and so forth. It was actually almost dangerous going from the greens to the tees, everybody whacking you on the back and yelling. But it was great fun. And, of course, you have to throw in the '86 Masters.

Those wonderful receptions will always stay with me, and I'm grateful to the people of Scotland that I was able to experience such warmth one last time.

2005: *the* MEDAL *of* FREEDOM

AS I LOOK BACK OVER THE YEARS AT ALL THE WONDERFUL THINGS PEOPLE HAVE DONE FOR ME, I get quite emotional. I deeply appreciate each and every occasion, and I'm always humbled. It's overwhelming to think about, really. I've had parades in my honor, been given keys to cities, and have received honorary degrees. I've had plaques installed at a couple of courses commemorating memorable shots in my career. And I had a bronze plaque erected in my honor at Augusta National Golf Club, which, considering my love for Augusta, was awfully special. Such gestures have touched me beyond words, and it shows how truly thoughtful people can be.

Perhaps more important than all of them, however, is the Presidential Medal of Freedom, which I received last fall from President George W. Bush. Established by the executive order of President John F. Kennedy in 1963, the Medal of Freedom is our country's highest civil award. To be included in the company of those who have been honored in the past, and those who were honored with me, is something very special and greatly appreciated.

The ceremony was held at the White House on November 9, 2005, and it was a day I will never forget. When I walked in, there was a nice lady taking pictures of all the guests, and I didn't quite recognize her right away with the camera hiding her face. I knew the voice, though, and what a voice she has: it was Aretha Franklin. I talked with Carol Burnett and Paul Harvey; I've known Paul for a long time. I met Robert Conquest, the author, and Alan Greenspan was there. I went up and shook hands with Muhammad Ali. I had first met him in 1996 at the PGA Championship at Valhalla Golf Club in Louisville. I was delighted to see him again.

During the ceremony I sat between Frank Robinson, the baseball Hall-of-Famer and manager of the Washington Nationals, and General Richard B. Myers, who had recently retired as President Bush's chairman of the Joint Chiefs of Staff. Just before we sat down, Frank's wife came up to me

and said that the one thing Frank wanted to do was to play Augusta National Golf Club. I told her I could take care of that, that it would be my pleasure. In fact, I'm still waiting on Frank to call me so we can set that up.

When I talked with Dick Myers, I was curious how President Bush was to work for. I didn't know quite how to ask it, but he was just great. He gave me an example of the way things are done. He said, "We would go to a meeting and all of us would sit together and discuss what has to be done with a certain situation. Once we all came to a consensus and made a decision, you never had to watch your back. We always tried to do what we thought was right, but whether we were

Receiving the Medal of Freedom from President Bush in 2005 was an extremely emotional moment for me.

right or wrong, he always stood by us and supported us." It's always interesting to hear how our leaders approach the problems they face, how our government works, how they meet challenges. In a democracy such as ours, we should know what's going on—that's our duty as citizens.

I had visited the White House and met with President Bush earlier in the year, just after my last Masters. Gary Player and I visited him at the White House as part of the promotional run-up of events before the Presidents Cup in Prince William County, Virginia, which I'm happy to say we won, although I'm more proud to say that the game of golf itself won because of the way both teams competed—with equal amounts of effort and sportsmanship. The proper spirit in which the matches were contested was a pleasure to see. It was a pleasure to meet with the president again, and on such a meaningful occasion. I think Mom and Dad would have been quite proud.

To be included in the company of those who have been honored in the past, and those who were honored with me, is something very special and greatly appreciated.

I have to say it was an equal pleasure meeting the other honored guests at the ceremony; they all were just wonderful. What a wide variety of talented folks! They were great to be around, and obviously, they all had done some meaningful things in their lives. I think we all felt the same way: that this was a tremendous honor and it was, without a doubt, a very memorable day.

the joys of COACHING

ONE WAY FOR ME TO SPEND MORE TIME WITH MY CHILDREN, even as I chased a little white ball around golf courses all over the world, was to get involved in their activities. One of the most enjoyable activities, for me, was helping out as a coach whenever possible.

As much as I wanted to, I never took the job of being a head coach because I had to travel so much, but I was always willing to act as an assistant coach, and I tried to do that with all five of my kids in whatever sports they were involved in. Mostly I tended to lend a hand on football

I enjoy coaching, but I especially like working with my sons, such as this lesson from 1983 with Jackie and Gary (right).

and baseball teams, but both Barb and I always sought other ways we could help out, like Barb assuming duties as an official scorer at school basketball games.

I've been asked if my presence at a practice or a sports event affected the things going on. I honestly don't know if it affected the competition; I hope it didn't. But I remember Chris Smith, who played golf at Ohio State University with my son Gary and who plays on the PGA Tour, saying once that he liked to see me out on the golf course when Ohio State had a match. He and the other players for the Buckeyes were used to me being around, while the other team surely wasn't.

As for whether or not my being there affected my children, well, they just had to deal with it. I remember telling my dad once that I got a little uptight when he was following me around the golf course during junior tournaments, and his response was basically: "Too bad." He wanted to be there and support me, and I was simply going to have to get used to it. My feelings were identical when it came to my own kids, and now with my grandkids. Currently, we have nineteen, and you can imagine how Barb and I might be running from one game to the next and the next.

I remember telling my dad once that I got a little uptight when he was following me around the golf course during junior tournaments, and his response was basically: "Too bad."

Truthfully, I never gave much thought to what my impact could possibly be, except that I wanted it to be positive. I was just another dad helping; I was a fixture around the place, and that's all I wanted to be. There was also enough kid in me that I just enjoyed hanging around. Occasionally, while the kids would be off going through football drills that I couldn't assist with, I would take a kicking tee and go down to one end of the field and kick field goals. I'd start at twenty yards and keep moving back. For a while I could still make some fifty-yarders.

FAMILY

THROUGHOUT MY COMPETITIVE CAREER, there was really only one fundamental principle that carried me through, from the day I became a professional golfer to the day last year when I retired. It kept me focused, helped me put problems in perspective, facilitated my ability to concentrate on the golf course, and allowed me to reach my potential. It could be summed up in two words: family first.

When Barbara and I decided to start a family, first with Jackie, when I was still an amateur, and then followed by Steve, Nan, Gary, and Michael, all other matters in life took a backseat. Sure, I wanted to be the best golfer I could, and I wanted to provide for my family, but I never let golf or anything else consume me to the point where I didn't have time to spend with my family. In terms of order of importance, it was always family first, followed by golf, business, and then my own recreation. If golf had ever seriously threatened my family life, I would have quit cold.

Golf is a game, and it's a good game, and I wouldn't be writing this book if it weren't for the game and the things I was able to do on a golf course. But golf wasn't the only thing in my life.

This Golf Family of the Year award from 1986 is one of my most cherished possessions.

Eighteen professional majors is a record I'm proud of, but Barbara and the kids are the best things that ever happened to me.

Some people may have thought I was fanatical about my devotion to my family. I made it a point that I would never be gone more than two weeks at a time, and often I would hop on a plane after a tournament round and fly home for one of the kids' games, or another function that I didn't want to miss, and then I would fly back the next day in time for the following round. Was I fanatical? Well, if you can't be fanatical about your family, if you can't put them first, then what does that say about your priorities?

Do I think I could have been a better player if I would have pushed everything else aside and focused on golf? Maybe. But do I think I would have missed something in life? There's no question

Steve (left) and Jackie started golf early—this picture was taken in 1966.

in my mind. I'm far happier having my five kids and my nineteen grandkids than to be worrying about the number of trophies I can put on a mantel. There has to be a balance in your life, and just as I did in balancing my schedule, I balanced golf against being the best father I could be. I wanted to spend as much time with my children as my dad spent with me growing up. I had a very good role model to emulate.

I'm far happier having my five kids and my nineteen grandkids than to be worrying about the number of trophies I can put on a mantel.

As the kids grew, I was able to incorporate them more into the things I was doing. Obviously, one of those was having them caddie for me in tournaments. Even more enjoyable was having them as playing partners in various events, whether it was Steve in the AT&T Pebble Beach National Pro-Am, or Gary or Jackie in the Father-Son Challenge, or Michael in Johnny Miller's Pro-Am in Utah. Even when I prepared for major championships in my prime, the best days of preparation were when I could visit a major-championship site early, as was always my practice, and take the boys along and have them play with me. It was a blast watching them try to break 90 on a U.S. Open layout. I enjoyed it more than they did.

In my prime I missed a lot of what might be considered by other people to be normal Sundays. I was always working on Sundays, which, if you're a golfer, that's what you want, or you're not earning a living. Now that I'm not part of the competitive golf scene anymore, we've begun to fill our Sundays with a new tradition that I'm enjoying thoroughly. All five kids have lived within a couple of miles of Barbara and me, and that says a lot about how close our family is. A couple of years ago we started having the kids over on Sundays with their families for dinner. Many families around the world do that; we never had that chance because most Sundays I was working. It has been wonderful. I've enjoyed having the kids and the grandkids over and having the

In 1973 I won my third straight Walt Disney World Open.

house be torn apart. I watch them like a hawk because I never know where they're going to be or what they're going to get into. It's a riot, and I look forward to it every week.

Golf isn't even a part of the equation. A few of the grandchildren are old enough now to have taken up an interest in the game, which is great, but my grandkids never ask me about golf or what I did. They ask me if they can have a popsicle or a drink.

I was asked at my final British Open last year what I thought my legacy might be. I don't know, and, really, that's out of my control. I think fans and members of the media will probably determine that. I'm not really concerned about what my legacy is in relation to the game of golf. I'm more concerned about what my legacy is with my family. If I've done it properly, and I can hold my head up to my wife and kids and grandkids, that's the most important thing.

Left: It was a true joy having Jackie caddie for me in this 1982 U.S. Open practice round at Pebble Beach. Above: The Nicklaus family, March, 2006.

AFTERWORD

I MAY HAVE CEASED PLAYING GOLF COMPETITIVELY IN 2005, but that really only ended one facet of the game that I have enjoyed for more than half a century. To me there were few things in life more enjoyable than championship golf, and for a long time nothing, besides my family, gave me more satisfaction. That period in my life is over now. The enjoyment of playing golf went hand in hand with being competitive. Once that ceased, once I could no longer do something that I once did well, it lost a bit of its glow.

Over the last couple of years I've started to spend more time doing other things rather than preparing to play golf, and frankly, I've really enjoyed it. I think when I plan to go someplace, I can go do what I want to and not worry about getting organized for the next golf game. I know my body likes it.

I've never been one who looks back, unless asked, but looking back over these pages only reinforces the idea that the game of golf brought out the best in me and provided me with so many wonderful memories. Do I mind looking back now? It's the only thing I have anymore. I don't have anything to look forward to, as it relates to golf. When I was in competition and trying to play, to me looking back was not the right way to approach the game. But as you get older, you get a little bit more sentimental about things, more nostalgic, so I look back on it, and it's all right. I look back at my record and figure it wasn't too bad.

I had my day, and now it's time to let the next generation have their day. I'm well aware that people might expect me to remain involved in golf, and looking ahead, I can promise you that will always be the case, given my love for golf course design and my commitment to putting on one of the best tournaments in the world at the Memorial Tournament. Aside from that, I've let people know that I'll be around if I'm needed. I mean that, too. I would always welcome any opportunity to contribute. I won't go sticking my nose into things, but if someone thinks that my input might be helpful in solving a problem or dealing with a certain issue, then I'd be happy to oblige. After all, it's not like I've ever had trouble expressing an opinion.

As I move on I'd have to say that, by and large, the game is in good hands. I'm looking forward to new challenges. I look forward to spending time with my kids and grandkids, and after so many years of doing things I wanted to do, it's time I did things with Barb that she might want to do. I think we all should do what we want to do, if we are fortunate enough to have that luxury.

Would I like to do it all again? Of course I would. It was all tremendous fun and very rewarding. I think we'd all like to be twenty or thirty years younger, but that's not going to happen. I'm fortunate to say that I don't feel a great need to go back. People have asked me what I would do differently. Frankly, I can't think of a single thing.

ACKNOWLEDGMENTS

ANY UNDERTAKING OF THIS MAGNITUDE REQUIRES THE CONCERTED EFFORTS OF A GREAT MANY PEOPLE, either directly or behind the scenes, and I am grateful to all the people who had a hand in making this a successful venture and one I that have enjoyed.

As always, I have to start with my wife, Barbara, who has been my partner in all my endeavors, and who always manages to put a finer point on a given task. Of course, it was Barbara, my mother, Helen, and my sister, Marilyn, who were so instrumental in making the Jack Nicklaus Museum happen with their tireless accounting and caretaking of the many mementos and artifacts that are housed within. I could never thank them enough for their love, support, and dedication on my behalf.

With respect to the museum, I also want to recognize curator Steve Auch, and his predecessor Gerald Goodson, as well as John Hines, Lee Lockhart, and Barbara Hartley. And a special thanks to The Ohio State University for their support of and commitment to the museum.

I would be remiss in not acknowledging my support team at the Nicklaus Companies for their hands-on efforts, as well as those from the International Management Group who got behind this project. Finally, thanks to David Shedloski for his collaborative energy, and a big thank-you to all the folks at becker&mayer! for bringing to life in these pages the stories that have made up my life and career.

PHOTO CREDITS

Images and removable facsimiles on the following pages appear courtesy of the Jack Nicklaus Museum, with photography by Fred Vuich: 19, 22, 29, 31, 37, 38, 40, 42, 47, 51, 53, 57, 60, 61, 67, 72, 73, 83, 86, 95, 96, 97, 98, 103, 105, 114, 115, 117, 118, 122, 126, 135, 139, 140, 145, 149, 152, 154, 155, 157, 166, 168.

Page 2: © Bettmann/CORBIS
Page 5: © Tony Roberts/CORBIS
Page 7: Steve Powell/Getty Images
Page 10-11: Fred Vuich/Sports Illustrated
Page 12: Nicklaus Family Archives/Jack Nicklaus Museum
Page 13: Bill Foley/The Columbus Dispatch
Page 15: Bill Foley/Jack Nicklaus Museum
Page 16: Ollie Atkins Photographs, Special Collections & Archives, George Mason University
Page 17: Jack Nicklaus Museum
Page 21: Ollie Atkins Photographs, Special Collections & Archives, George Mason University
Page 24: Bill Foley/Jack Nicklaus Museum
Page 26: George Silk/Time Life Pictures/ Getty Images
Page 32: Bill Foley/Jack Nicklaus Museum
Page 35: Dick Davis/Rocky Mountain News/Polaris
Page 41: AP/Wide World Images
Page 43: Ollie Atkins Photographs, Special Collections & Archives, George Mason University
Page 45: AP/Wide World Images
Page 49: AP/Wide World Images
Page 50: Historic Golf Photos
Page 55: © Bettmann/CORBIS
Page 56: Historic Golf Photos
Page 58: Courtesy of Francine Cherry
Page 59: AP/Wide World Images
Page 64: Courtesy of Firestone Country Club
Page 66: © Reuters/CORBIS
Page 68: Marvin Newman/Sports Illustrated
Page 70-71: © Bettmann/CORBIS
Page 74: Historic Golf Photos
Page 76-77: Harry How/Getty Images
Page 78: AP/Wide World Images
Page 80: AP/Wide World Images

Page 84: Ray Matjasic © 8/12/1973 The Plain Dealer. All rights reserved. Reprinted with permission.
Page 89: AP/Wide World Images
Page 92: AP/Wide World Images
Page 94: AP/Wide World Images
Page 99: Dom Furore/Golf Digest
Page 100: Nicklaus Family Archives/Jack Nicklaus Museum
Page 104: AP/Wide World Images
Page 107: © Bettmann/CORBIS
Page 108: Bill Foley/Jack Nicklaus Museum
Page 111: Jack Nicklaus Museum
Page 112: Bill Foley/Jack Nicklaus Museum
Page 113: Mike Fiala/AFP/Getty Images
Page 116: Brian Morgan
Page 121: Brian Morgan
Page 123: © Bettmann/CORBIS
Page 125: Historic Golf Photos
Page 128: David Cannon/Allsport/Getty Images
Page 132: Dave Maxwell/AFP/Getty Images
Page 134: AP/Wide World Images
Page 138: Courtesy of Larry Phillips Photography
Page 141: Nicklaus Design (removable plan)
Page 142: Jim Mandeville/Jack Nicklaus Companies
Page 146: Historic Golf Photos
Page 156: © Eddie Keogh/Reuters/CORBIS
Page 157: Courtesy of R&A Championships Limited (removable scorecard)
Page 159: Steve Powell/Allsport/Getty Images
Page 162: AP/Wide World Images
Page 164: Brian Morgan/Getty Images
Page 167: Life Magazine
Page 170: © Bettmann/CORBIS
Page 171: Jim Mandeville/Jack Nicklaus Companies
Page 176: © Mike Blake/Reuters/CORBIS